Hope, Wisdom and Courage

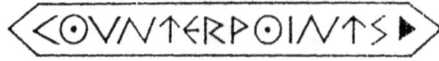

COUNTERPOINTS

Studies in Criticality

Series Editor
Shirley R. Steinberg

Vol. 559

Hope, Wisdom and Courage

Teaching and Learning Practices in
Today's Schools and Beyond

Edited by
Susan Groundwater-Smith

PETER LANG

New York · Berlin · Bruxelles · Chennai · Lausanne · Oxford

Library of Congress Cataloging-in-Publication Data

Names: Groundwater-Smith, Susan, editor.
Title: Hope, wisdom and courage : teaching and learning practices in
today's schools and beyond / Edited by Susan Groundwater-Smith.
Description: New York, NY : Peter Lang, [2025] | Series: Counterpoints,
1058–1634 ; vol 559 | Includes bibliographical references.
Identifiers: LCCN 2024042344 (print) | LCCN 2024042345 (ebook) |
ISBN 9781636676906 (paperback) | ISBN 9781636676883 (pdf) |
ISBN 9781636676890 (epub)
Subjects: LCSH: Teaching–Philosophy. | Teachers–Conduct of life. |
Learning–Philosophy. | Education and globalization. | Education–Aims
and objectives.
Classification: LCC LB1025.3 .H673 2025 (print) | LCC LB1025.3 (ebook) |
DDC 371.102–dc23/eng/20241024
LC record available at https://lccn.loc.gov/2024042344
LC ebook record available at https://lccn.loc.gov/2024042345
DOI 10.3726/b22391

Bibliographic information published by the Deutsche Nationalbibliothek.
The German National Library lists this publication in the German
National Bibliography; detailed bibliographic data is available
on the Internet at http://dnb.d-nb.de.

Cover design by Peter Lang Group AG

ISSN 1058-1634 (print)
ISBN 9781636676906 (paperback)
ISBN 9781636676883 (ebook)
ISBN 9781636676890 (epub)
DOI 10.3726/b22391

© 2025 Peter Lang Group AG, Lausanne
Published by Peter Lang Publishing Inc., New York, USA
info@peterlang.com – www.peterlang.com

This publication has been peer reviewed.

CONTENTS

LEARNING FROM ESSAYS ON HOPE, WISDOM AND COURAGE IN TODAY'S SCHOOLS AND BEYOND

Susan Groundwater-Smith

This introductory essay serves several purposes. Essentially, the essay argues that it is taking a constitutive approach in that the language form that is employed affects the ways in which particular phenomena and practices are understood and embraced. Its semantic structure both shapes, expands and limits the ways in which we can envisage the world of which we are all a part.

It is designed as a 'thought experiment' that requires of its readers, inclusive of a range of stakeholders in education, to change their expectations of what ordinarily constitutes an academic chapter. It asks them to engage with a somewhat different form of communication: a critical essay. It seeks the use of the imagination that will create new mental models that can link hope, courage and wisdom in our schools and beyond. This introduction foreshadows the essays that follow. All are sensitive to the many global, economic, societal and environmental discourses so dominant in the public domain. These act as antidotes to the more pernicious influences that those discourses have on educational policy making and practice.

Why the essay?

Apart from my early years spent in the Orkney Islands I lived through my childhood in a terrace house on Upper Addison Gardens in Kensington, London. The street ran off Addison Road and was named after Joseph Addison, a great essayist, who along with Richard Steele, established a new literary form. Many of their essays were published in their jointly produced journal, *The Spectator*, in the first decades of the 18th century. The writing, particularly that of Addison, was breezy, pithy and conversational in contrast to the rather stuffy epistles of the day. Written in an active and clear voice, pieces captured the essence of the age and the times, ranging from observations on love, theatre and even the making of gardens. Each acted to provoke, some even to enrage. Perhaps it is an exaggerated claim to suggest that living in this place engendered my own love of the essay.

For me the essay form re-shapes what chapters in academic texts ordinarily do. The essays in this collection, embrace a creative narrative style infused with the carefully considered illuminative perspective of each essayist. The result is idiosyncratic rather than academic, bound as the latter is by specific conventions regarding scholarly work. As Norman (2019: p. 1) notes:

> This concern for the concrete, for realistic complexity rather than rationalistic reduction, is why an essay, like a poem, ultimately is its style – and why essayism is itself a style . . .

To read Virginia Woolf's essay 'Street haunting: A London Adventure', for example, is to enter into the cognisance of an extraordinary writer, free to use a language of nuance, ambiguity and uncertainty.

The scope of the essay gives the writer permission to explore: events and feelings; love and loss; the particular and the general; romance and satire; the ideal and the everyday. Whether Michel de Montaigne writing on cannibals or Jonathan Swift on consuming Irish babies, the essay is a compelling form. In this book its cultural vectors cross and re-cross the landscape of educational practices both within and beyond schools. Dillon (2018, p. 13, p. 97) writes of essays approaching their subjects 'slantwise' and being a 'solid thing made fully present on the page and then dissolving in all else it implies'; in this way they allow the authors a range of possibilities and arguments to imagine, to repudiate and re-consider the subject matter.

Our subject matter, embracing as it does, hope, courage and wisdom, has undoubtedly been considered through numerous publications involving the many disciplines that make up the field of education, in particular that which applies to schooling, but also taking account of learning outside the classroom. However, it is our desire to engage with what Addison called the pleasures of the imagination that allows for the emergence of ideas. Ideas that have the capacity to surprise, to stimulate, to transform, even to antagonise. These writings should not be confused with opinion pieces designed to persuade, but rather reflections to be evaluated. They eschew nailing down those concrete matters that are demanded by the language of performativity, governed as it is only by that which is measurable.

The essays contained in this book take a constitutive approach: The essay form itself both shapes and limits the experience of the readers as they share in the construction of the text. They offer both a linguistic and philosophical tool with which to read the various texts. They eschew the endless lists of citations that may act to interrupt engagement with the many rich, divergent and illuminative ideas contained in them. As well, they decry the borrowing and adoption of an inappropriate language arising from business practices in a global world of neo-liberalism. Richard Pring, the British philosopher of education, draws upon the oft-cited Wittgenstein aphorism that we can be bewitched by the mis-use of language. He sees that there is an Orwellian flavour to much of the social policies, such as education, employed by governments and their agencies.

Typically, academic papers or chapters are written in a manner that may exclude and marginalise those who are not immersed in the specific specialised area. This is particularly problematic for many of the stakeholders in education who bear the consequences of the policies and practices in which they have little voice, such as many students, their teachers and their parents and/or caregivers who are, nonetheless burdened with them. Therefore, these essays do not seek either to supplement or supplant traditional academic work but rather to make possible a different dialogue between writers and readers. If the genre of the essay has the capacity to affect the ways in which we perceive and engage with the world then it has a remarkable power to address anew, matters that have been leached out of the education enterprise. Hope, courage and wisdom have been largely effaced by the neo-liberal language of globalisation, pragmatism, productivity and competition. These essays are an antidote.

Why hope, courage and wisdom?

In my Harold Wyndham memorial address to the New South Wales Institute of Educational Research (NSWIER) 2022[1] I commenced with an extract from Emily Dickinson's fragile and delicate poem on 'hope': 'Hope' is the thing with feathers / That perches in the soul / And sings the tune without the words / And never stops / At all. It is a salutary reminder, in an era where policies and practices in education are under unceasing assault, that we should see hope as an existential force that can enable these challenges to be faced with vitality and energy.

All the same, 'Hope,' the great Czech dissident playwright Václav Havel wrote,

> is not the same as joy that things are going well, or willingness to invest in enterprises that are obviously headed for early success, but, rather, an ability to work for something because it is good, not just because it stands a chance to succeed. (1986, pp. 181–182)

Here Havel distinguishes hope from superficial optimism. Hope is grounded in the goodness of what is desired. It rests upon wisdom, a specific form of discursive ethical discourse. In education those who have hope yearn for a change from the circumstances where teachers are poorly paid and overworked and teaching is overgoverned. Instead they wish for conditions that respect and reward the most complex conditions of practice.

To do 'good' is to re-energise practice, in the words of Santoro (2018) to 'remoralise', to recognise the moral centre of practice. In her investigations of the demoralisation of teachers Santoro argued that demoralisation occurs when teachers 'can no longer engage in what they consider good work' (p. 175). Doing 'good work' is not a solitary charitable activity and is not in the possession of one individual but is in the context of practice, governed by practitioners as members of communities functioning collectively: able to enquire and reflect upon the conditions of practice; to identify where it may be possible to 'do good'; and, to celebrate circumstances where this may happen.

As an illumination of one educational practice built upon 'the good' I choose to cite the work of a young Australian school teacher, Sarah Donnelly (2022) who took an appointment, as a primary school teacher, in a remote country town in New South Wales. It is a town that has been characterised as dangerous and dysfunctional, to be avoided, rather than visited. In her time there Sarah built up a remarkable relationship with her students by making deep connections with them, their families and Indigenous elders. She centred her teaching and learning based on the local environment and its history in ways that enhanced and embraced local knowledges that too many had sought to efface. She explored sites of memory, local triumphs and tragedies.

Her mantra with her students was that mistakes are expected, respected, inspected and corrected. Her fortitude and courage contributed to many innovations that supported learning during the difficult years of drought and later the isolation of all during the COVID years of on-line learning. Sarah used the full capacity of her creative potential by re-inventing her teaching self as one with agency, in contrast to being a mere factotum, a functionary, carrying through the will of others. Nowhere does the account, rich and informed as it is, refer to test results, performativity, teaching standards – all common parlance in the writing of teachers' work.

With 'hope' at our backs it is now incumbent upon us to survey what lies beneath today's educational landscape, including its surface features and its morphology. We need to explore further teacher agency in these tumultuous times and some of the challenges and vicissitudes teachers face in relation to the adoption of particular forms of research evidence and the ways in which it can undergird or undermine professional practice and influence the ways in which teaching is seen and the ways in which teachers see themselves. Teachers such as Sarah Donnelly, are their own best 'inspectors' relying on reflexive self-insight, employing evaluation and action research as a powerful force for their professional learning that, in turn, should inform the esteem in which they are held. All of this takes a particular kind of courage. For to be 'good' is not only to be wise, but to have courage.

Courage is inevitably related to risk. In effect, as a disposition, it has to do with volitional behaviour, a willingness to be audacious under the veil of uncertainty. In a keynote address to education graduates in 2008, I drew attention to the collective courage of Norwegian teachers during the Quisling era during World War 2 (named after the pro-Nazi Norwegian leader at the time). In the face of an attempt to 'nazify' the curriculum, teachers resisted at the risk of their own lives. Certainly, many instances can be cited since then, but the force of the Norwegian case lies in its direct relation to education and policy decisions that the teachers so bravely and at great cost, refused to accept. Teachers who had hope for a better future took their community with them.

Courage faces fear with a determination to act. It requires the employment of an ethical sensibility in exercising judgment wisely in order to address those constraints that lead to injustice and to harm. Courage cannot sit lightly on the shoulders of those engaged in the educational enterprise. There are many 'we know best' forces arrayed against them; determined to argue that this or that practice is 'best practice' and that this or that accountability measure is deemed the 'best measure'. Resistance is risky business.

Taking risks is not to be engaged with lightly. To assess and judge the costs and the beneficial outcomes requires a degree of wisdom. Biesta (2017) in his exploration of the future of teaching and teacher education regards much of the current onslaught upon teachers, their practices and preparation, as a means to de-professionalise them, to command and control them. He turns instead to an argument for teacher judgment and discernment – that is, for the capacity of teachers to exercise informed, practical wisdom in order to act thoughtfully, effectively and ethically, employing all their critical faculties.

This book is designed to reanimate a positive set of dispositions regarding hope, wisdom and courage. Each of the essays that follow suggests pathways forward.

The sting of words

These essays are an invitation. Each embodies a language that grounds its readers in a specific discourse with which to engage, at times disrupting the ways in which we have focussed upon education in the past. Each one asks us to take notice. They are paper bound in a particular order, but readers may choose for themselves where to start and where to finish. The search for the writers has been to find a means that can bring hope, courage and wisdom to life, that can sting the readers into fresh considerations that transcend what has been too long seemingly self-evident and commonplace.

It is worth heeding the Oxford Dictionary in its indication that the word 'essay' is closely related to 'assay' – to put to the test. Our essayists, with their diverse histories of experience in education in schools and beyond, are ready to be put to the test themselves, but also desire to put the readers to the test in exploring and exploding cherished ideas and beliefs.

What follows is not only a range of responses to the invitation to reflect upon hope, courage and wisdom in education today but also a variety of formats. It was not my intention as editor to set out a formula for contributors to follow, but rather provide conditions for writers to structure and make their arguments in their own fashion. Some take us directly into the matter at hand in the form of an aphorism marking off the territory to be explored; others are exploratory travelling around the margins of that which perplexes and even confounds the writer.

Where to begin?

It has already been suggested that this collection, bound as it is in a volume, does not necessarily presage the order within which it should be read. But I, as a reader, discovered for myself a certain route through the series, with one eye cocked to the way in which I might find the landmarks. I am not suggesting that one essay has more gravitas than another but would rather propose that each raises fresh questions, even uncertainties. Each is an invention of its writer(s). But that is not the end of the matter, for in reading each is also an invention of its reader; a fragment that will attach itself to what is already known and understood, or misunderstood. There is no singular reading, but there is a risk of hasty reading – of skimming the ideas, accepting or rejecting them. This collection invites slow reading, rumination and reflection.

The first two essays, those of Ian Menter and Stephen Kemmis bring to attention, among other matters, the exercise of wisdom. For Ian it is the wisdom of adopting resources for hope by exploring the theoretical work of two powerful and profound social theorists, Raymond Williams and Paulo Friere, both of whom were disturbed by 'the perils of populism and performativity'. He points the reader to a society that requires high quality education as an essential foundation for democracy and freedom.

Stephen identifies the wisdom of seeking to explore beneath the surface; to find the hidden life of education in the everyday. As sentient human beings people are always learning. He argues that 'Education does not stand still. It realises shared *hopes* for people and the world: shared hopes that it can serve the individual and collective interests of everyone it touches'. In his ruminations he holds out hope for educational practitioners to go on in their practice contributing to the formation of individuals and society in ways that are just and inclusive.

Courage lies at the heart of Catherine Burke's essay, as an historian she draws upon possibilities from past and present practices to imagine a more liberatory form of schooling, giving greater agency to learners as they develop curiosity and excitement around their learning. Her narrative embraces an encounter with a very different view of schooling, one that sees the impact of school lockdowns during the COVID pandemic. Her argument rests on the premise that the disturbances to what had become solidified material and temporal conditions for teaching and learning might be seen as opportunities to imagine a very different educational regime.

A theme in relation to learner agency is at the heart of Eve Mayes' essay, written with Natasha Abhaywickama and Emma Heyink is learner agency. She moves between her own encounters with young people regarding climate activism in the context of schooling to drawing out a wider portrayal of the 'mass mobilisation of young people, who collectively refused the political and pedagogical status quo demanding bold and transformative action to address the climate crisis'. Resonating with Stephen Kemmis' hidden life of education she identifies teaching and learning spaces beyond school classrooms as being those where there is a quest for climate justice – a journey that takes young people and their teachers into existential territories where they interrogate their foundational assumptions, with lasting impact upon pedagogies, curriculum and systems.

Sharing a concern regarding the insidious and negative impacts of neo-liberalism on every aspect of teaching and learning practices in today's schools (and even beyond) Barry Down and Alan Reid make a case for a restored social imaginary. They build upon a greater and more human understanding of educative practices that require participative consent. Barry draws upon his extensive experiences in a variety of contexts that have informed his developing and never complete activism. Like Ian Menter he has identified key writers who have influenced his own thinking and practices and mourns that development of school education as wholly instrumental around the needs of human capital formation including 'job readiness, skills formation, vocationalisation, curriculum differentiation, qualifications and credentials, career guidance and discipline'. From his critique he moves towards propositions that could inform practices that embody hope, courage and wisdom.

Using Australia as a case study Alan Reid turns to ways in which a democratic renewal could act as an antidote to the prevailing corporate managerialism. He traces the current demise of the democratic impulse to a range of factors including: 'institutional processes; a weakening of political equality; and, the debasement of political culture in the public sphere'. He aspires to establishing a sustainable curriculum and pedagogy aimed at authentic civics education by engaging what he names as a 'thick' version of democracy that requires 'citizens to actively engage with democratic life'. Like Eve Mayes and Catherine Burke he appeals to the principle of engagement with student voice as the consequential stakeholders in the schooling enterprise.

Putting young people at the heart of the enterprise of schooling has been the focus of Linda O'Brien's aspiration for a 'pedagogy of hope'. As a school principal she has supported and led multiple, interconnected strategies that mitigate against those narrow and instrumental policies so decried by Barry and Allen. The case which Linda spells out is informed by her deep and personal commitment to her students, many of whom face challenging and difficult circumstances. With the theories of Pierre Bourdieu as her signposts and her knowledge of the social and economic conditions of her students she has led her teachers and her community to formulate a way forward that is hopeful and enriching, creative and exciting for all who participate.

Also turning to democracy and concerns for inclusiveness, the themes so prominent in these essays, Kylie Captain and Catherine Burgess bring to the fore the particular challenge of providing conditions of hope for First Nation's People through the powerful avenue of truth telling. By drawing attention to the need to dismantle the prevailing legal, material and historical assumptions underlying the colonial history of Australia taught in the nation's schools, they inject an element of hope and optimism. They build upon 'Country Centred Relationships' where the Aboriginal and Torres Strait Islander voice is listened to and engaged with, thus contributing to a longed-for change. Their powerful essay concludes with an injunction for teachers to be brave: 'This requires us to get out of our own way, set our egos aside and be vulnerable in a place we are normally in control of'.

The final two essays in the collection are clearly not the last word, but each takes us well beyond today's schools. Jane Hunter and Jorge Knijnik concern themselves with learning regarding gender equality through different organisational structures and practices. Using as a touchstone the United Nation's Sustainable Goal number 5, regarding gender equality they suggest that there is a prevailing fear that it is unattainable; until, that is, they turn to their two telling cases. One of these is the participation of young people from a small Indigenous community, Borroloola, in a tour associated with the World Cup in Brazil, 2014 where girls played a significant role; the other the 2023 Women's World Cup international event devoted entirely to women. Each of these leaves a legacy that contributes to a Frierian dialogue that can influence a genuine social transformation. They agree that this an aspiration not yet fully realised in terms of gender equality but one where genuine progress has been made through the agency of social learning.

Remy Low's is a different trajectory, but like all the essays in this collection intersects with its key themes, in particular that of courage. Drawing upon the imaginative power required to write speculative texts, indeed the very nature of the essays in this collection, he takes us beyond the oppressive circumstances that can prevail not only in marginalised communities, but indeed in an increasingly challenging and stressful world. To achieve this end he draws upon the work of a Bengali feminist educator whose dream for girls' education was actualised in spite of a censorial and difficult environment. However, using Sartre as a guide, Remy's essay is not solely a narrative of Rokeya's initiatives, it also highlights the liberation to be found in speculative writing and its impact upon the many stresses to be found in our problematic contemporary world.

Conclusion

Each of these essays has been written with the intention to provoke dialogue and debate just as was the case in the days of Addison and Steele, my original inspiration. Our particular purpose in this collection of essays is to reinstate the language of hope, courage and wisdom into the lexicon of education. It is to be hoped that readers examine their own ambitions to identity and act on a range of such practices.

On the back cover of Susan Sontag's collection of essays and speeches *At the Same Time* Sontag (2007) three hand written sentences are repeated, 'Do something, Do something, Do something'. It is sincerely hoped that these contributions may lead beyond thought, to action, to do something about education today.

Note

1 The NSWIER has given me permission to quote drawing upon the address that has only been published to its members.

References

Biesta, G. (2017). The future of teacher education: Evidence, competence or wisdom? In M. Peters, B. Cowie, & I. Menter (Eds.), *A companion to research in teacher education* (pp. 435–453). Springer.

Dillon, B. (2018). *Essayism: On form, feeling and non-fiction*. Fitzcarraldo Editions.

Donnelly, S. (2022). *Big things grow: A memoir of teaching on Country in Wilcannia*. Allen & Unwin.

Havel, V. (1986). *Disturbing the peace*. Vintage Books.

Norman, M. (2019, January 8). What essays are and what essayists do. *Public Books*. https://www.publicbooks.org/top-10-2019-what-essays-are-and-what-essayists-do/

Santoro, D. (2018). *Demoralised: Why teachers leave the profession they love and how they can stay*. Harvard Education Press.

Sontag, S. (2007). *At the same time: Essays and speeches*. Picador.

RESOURCES OF HOPE FOR EDUCATION IN THE 21ST CENTURY?

Ian Menter

Both Raymond Williams and Paolo Freire were born in 1921. While, so far as I am aware, the two men never met, they did share a deep commitment to human liberation, to equity and to justice. They were passionate socialists who brought their intellect and politics together to stimulate radical action in the disparate contexts in which they lived and worked. More than 100 years after their births, they may still inspire us to challenge the continuing threats to liberation, equity and justice that are so prevalent in the contemporary world, not least in the sphere of education. In particular we can find in their words some ways in which education may serve to underpin such challenges, indeed to provide 'resources of hope' (Williams) and 'a pedagogy of hope' (Freire).

During the 20th century not only were there two world wars (in the second of which Williams saw active service and in which nazism was defeated), but we also saw the ending of apartheid in South Africa, the collapse of the Berlin Wall and of the Soviet Union, as well as the demise of European empires and colonisation in many parts of the world. If each of these major events may be seen as significant moves towards greater democracy, it is deeply disturbing that during the final decades of that century global forces gave rise to the spread of 'neoliberalism', with a surge in populist governments and a series of economic crises which have led to austerity, poverty and greater inequity and injustice. Racism, misogyny and other forms of discrimination thrive, even in the most 'advanced' societies and autocrats lead countries in many parts of the world.

In addition to these threats to democracy we have also seen the continuation of destructive and murderous conflicts, such as those currently affecting Ukraine and Gaza where physical survival must be the prime aim for children and their families. There can be little hope for any conventional forms of education in such contexts. But the wider threat to all of us – even those of us not facing such violent conflict – is the ecological threat to the planet as a result of global warming. Our collective failure to achieve the necessary reductions in carbon emissions, puts the future of all species on the planet – including humanity – in serious doubt.

In this essay I seek to share the inspiration I have found from these two thinkers – Williams and Freire – in coming to understand and thereby to challenge some of these threats, as well as the constraints and oppressions brought about through the imposition of market-oriented and performative policies and practices on education systems across the world during the late 20th and early 21st centuries.

Williams, Freire and education

So what is it that a reading of Williams and Freire can tell us about education in the 21st century? Although they were both fundamentally optimists, they also shared deep concerns about the emerging neoliberal policies coming to dominate global politics towards the end of the 20th century. The perils of populism and performativity were predicted by both Williams and Freire, as we shall see. But they also shared – in their different ways – a commitment to public provision of high quality education as a necessary underpinning of democracy and freedom. In short they shared a deep humanism.

Williams grew up on the border between Wales and England and his first full length novel, *Border Country*, (Williams, 1960) is a largely autobiographical account of how he crossed not only geographical but also cultural and social borders during his lifetime. In my own recently published book *Raymond Williams and Education*, (Menter, 2022) I explore how his own biography – including grammar school in Abergavenny and studying at the University of Cambridge – shaped his insights and helped to inform his theoretical thinking.

Perhaps I can best summarise his understanding of education by quoting from another early book of his, *Communications*:

> I wish, first, that we should recognize that education is ordinary: that it is, before everything else, the process of giving to the ordinary members of society its full common meanings, and the skills that will enable them to amend these meanings, in the light of their personal and common experience. (1962/66, p. 14)

This book was developed from his input to a conference organised by the National Union of Teachers in the early 1960s. The commitment to permanent education was part of his vision of *The Long Revolution* (1961/2011), his belief – indeed hope – that in the 1960s Britain was becoming a more democratic, more inclusive, less class-differentiated society. Referring to the contribution education should make to these processes, he wrote:

> It is a question of whether we can grasp the real nature of our society, or whether we persist in social and educational patterns based on a limited ruling class, a middle professional class, a large operative class, cemented by forces that cannot be challenged and will not be changed. The privileges and barriers, of an inherited kind will, in any case go down. It is only a question of whether we replace them by the free play of the market, or by a public education designed to express and create the values of an educated democracy and a common culture. (Williams, 1961/2011, p. 76)

And then writing about his 'resources for a journey of hope' in the 1980s, in the early days of what became known as Thatcherism, the British version of neoliberalism, we have this:

> ... the objective changes which are now so rapidly developing are not only confusing and bewildering; they are also profoundly unsettling. The ways now being offered to live with these unprecedented dangers and these increasingly harsh dislocations are having many short-term successes and effects, but they are also in the long term, forms of further danger and dislocation. (Williams, 1983, p. 268)

Freire's ideas on education bear a remarkable similarity to Williams's. The first of his books to be published in English, *Cultural Action for Freedom* (Freire, 1972a), expressed how education itself – if properly provided – is a revolutionary and liberating process. Indeed his success in empowering rural populations in South America through adult literacy was the reason he was exiled. Education is a political process in Freire's conception.

In his second book, *Pedagogy of the Oppressed* (Freire, 1972b), he developed his critique of the 'banking concept' of education, that is the simplistic view of education as the transmission of pre-defined knowledge into the minds of the learner. He contrasted this with 'the problem-posing concept of education' which is a kind of social constructivist view of teaching and learning or what is today seen as a lynchpin of 'critical pedagogy'. His later work, *Pedagogy of Hope*, (Freire, 2014) is sub-titled *Reliving Pedagogy of the Oppressed* and is in essence Freire reflecting on many debates, discussions and criticisms he had encountered relating to this previous work. He strenuously refutes attempts to separate education and politics and suggests that hope is indeed an essential element of pedagogy – and I think many, if not all, teacher educators would recognise this and concur:

> One of the tasks of the progressive educator, through a serious, correct political analysis, is to unveil the opportunities for hope, no matter what the obstacles may be. After all, without hope, there is little we can do. (Freire, 1994, p. 3)

So, against the backdrop of these two sets of ideas, what is our sense of the current prospects for education, locally, regionally and globally? Where can we find evidence of the contribution that education may make to democratic, just and sustainable futures for citizens of the world? What indeed, and where, are our resources of hope in education?

Cultural materialism

In my own work analysing teacher education policy and practice I have found myself increasingly influenced and assisted by Williams's theoretical approach of cultural materialism. Expressed in the simplest way, this is the idea that social phenomena are best understood through recognising the interaction between the material world of production and the cultural world of human activity. The approach draws heavily on Marxian theory but avoids the kind of determinism that can 'dehumanise' some Marxist thought. It is perhaps best encapsulated in Williams's original concept of 'structures of feeling'. He first used this term when offering critical analyses of film and then developed it more fully in his discussions of literature. The term denotes the specific characteristics of a time and place depicted in a creative work, reflecting both the structural conditions which shape the experience of the participants as well as their subjective experience, their feelings. So, for example in education, we might encounter the interaction between a prescribed curriculum and the individual learning of a student. Or we may consider how the process of school inspection may impact on the lived experience of teachers in a particular school. These simple examples start to shed some light on how educational policy can impinge – whether positively or negatively – on the teaching and learning in schools and colleges.

Anthropological perspectives on education

Although Williams was not seen primarily as an educationist (although of course Freire was) nevertheless, as already indicated, he had a great deal to offer of value to educational studies. He is best known as a cultural theorist and throughout his life and work, as well as an active engagement in socialist politics, he explored the relationship between culture and society. That relationship is in essence what underpins the discipline of anthropology. Given the insights that the study of education can show about this relationship, it continues to astonish me how poorly the subject of anthropology is represented in university education departments around the world. Increasingly, for myself, in trying to make sense of teacher education in many parts of the world, I find I have been adopting an increasingly anthropological perspective. The study of teacher education within any society reveals much about the contemporary world and the changes we are experiencing. This should be no surprise to us for, if anthropology focusses on culture and in particular on the transmission of culture, then education must be a matter of central concern, for that is surely what education is – the transmission of culture, whether the educational processes are formal or informal. And teacher education provides the means by which teachers are prepared to play their part in these processes of transmission, the production and reproduction of cultures.

For many of the early scholars in anthropology from Margaret Mead to Mary Douglas, it has been all too obvious that the formation and development of the young members of a society is fundamental to understanding the norms, values and behaviours that prevail within that society. So, whether a society has developed formal systems of education or not, some of the deepest insights are to be gained from exploring how young people are shaped by their social environment. Furthermore, in 'advanced societies' what clearer indication of the formal expression of societal values, aspirations and hopes can there be than the approach taken to the preparation of teachers who have the societal responsibility for creating 'tomorrow's citizens'? Of course, the home, the family and community are also of great significance and the interaction between these and the formal education system must be a key focus for anthropological study.

Thus, I suggest, the education of teachers offers a key anthropological insight to societies. For me, this growing perception has arisen partly through an increasing involvement in comparative studies of teacher education. This perspective started to develop with my move very early in the 21st century from the peculiarities of the English (to borrow a phrase from E.P. Thompson) approach to teacher education to the very different but internationally more recognisable approach in Scotland. This was the beginning of a process continuing to this day of showing the significance of the connections between the nation state and teacher education.

However, in the context of neoliberalism encountered most dramatically in the western world the significance of these insights has also been recognised by politicians. In England, the United States, Australia and also in many 'developing' countries where globalisation has been having an impact, much political attention has been focussed on the preparation and training of teachers. Taking the country I know best, we have seen a steadily 'tightening grip' on teacher education policy in England since at least 1984, with the sustained attacks on educational theory and on the role of higher education in the provision. Teacher shortages have accelerated these processes with successive governments seeking to establish routes that are both quicker and cheaper for people to enter the teaching profession, but also a great expansion of less well qualified posts within the education system.

Deploying resources of hope in education

Where is the resistance to these destructive policies and practices to come from? What are the resources of hope that can be deployed and how can they be effective in 'turning back the tide'? As an educational researcher I would of course stress the importance of promoting and sustaining high quality research in, on and around education and teacher education (see Menter, 2023). The rise of increasingly functionalist closely controlled research activity has not assisted in revealing the underlying inequities and injustices promoted with much government policy. The need for independent and critical analysis of systems and processes has never been greater. Many years ago, Gerald Grace (1984) argued for 'critical policy scholarship' in the study of urban education. He argued for the need to recover 'a sense of the historical' and to confront the political and economic aspects of education, as well as the cultural and pedagogic. Since then, we have seen the further domination of educational research by approaches seeking 'quick fixes', 'magic bullets' and the like, what Grace described as a 'policy science' approach, often through the execution of randomised controlled trials, which rarely provide insights into the causes of educational failures and do little more than provide superficial insights. Yet in so far as governments invest in educational research, this tends to be where they put their money.

Following Grace's arguments from the 1980s, what is desperately needed are approaches which are based in a recognition of the impact of existing structures, their historical development and continuing influence on policies and on practices. This is where a cultural materialist approach can offer a much stronger basis for analysis than much of what is being undertaken today. Raymond Williams's analysis of the development of education in England, included in *The Long Revolution* demonstrates the power of taking such an approach. In tracing the historical influences on the emergence of public education he identifies three major forces that have struggled with each other to shape the provision of schooling. He called these three forces the 'old humanists', the 'public educators' and the 'industrial trainers'. With these three groupings reflecting respectively, the cultural, the political and the economic aims of education systems, there is not an education system in the world where such an analysis is not pertinent. Freire's adult literacy work in Brazil was fundamentally a public educator approach seeking to empower illiterate and oppressed people in rural settings. Such was the effectiveness of his work and the threat it posed towards capitalist economic development that he was exiled from the country. In England the struggles over curriculum and assessment – as well as the management of schools – that ensued from the 1988 Education Reform Act may also be understood as virulent interaction between the three forces. The tensions between the old humanists' arguments for a traditional curriculum, the public educators' emphasis on education for democracy, through a focus on literacy and numeracy, and the industrial trainers' arguments for training in technical skills and digital competence continue to play out into the 21st century.

In addition to this cultural materialist approach, as I suggested earlier, an anthropological perspective is also required. This was clearly understood by Freire as he responded to the ways in which people in rural Brazil were being exploited and oppressed through their lack of literacy and lack of education. Yet anthropology is a discipline that has not been significantly developed within educational studies, with just a few notable exceptions. What we have seen – but even this has been severely eroded in recent years – is what might be described as some anthropological influence on education studies through aspects of sociology. Before the foundation disciplines of educational studies were more or less expunged from teacher education in England, sociology had played a major part in helping student teachers to understand the significant influence of, for example, patterns of childcare and family life on children as learners. There has also been an adoption of ethnographic methods in educational studies, much of it borrowed from sociology and anthropology. These methods provided great insights from the 1970s onwards into the processes of differentiation and discrimination that were present in formal education systems including schooling and higher education. So anthropology may be seen to have made an important if indirect contribution to our understanding of education, but this has, as I have suggested, been largely expunged at least from education departments in universities over the past forty years or so. The situation is perhaps less extreme elsewhere, for example in the United States, parts of Europe, as well as China and Japan. In the United States one of the greatest contributions in this field has been from Kathryn Anderson-Levitt (2003, 2012) who has succeeded in drawing together scholars from many parts of the world to show the power of anthropological perspectives in understanding contemporary changes in education systems. Much of that work can also be seen to relate to the field of comparative education, a subject I myself studied during my own teacher education in the 1970s in England, but which has now completely disappeared from initial teacher education. But that subject does continue to exist, indeed thrives, through several journals as well as national and international scholarly societies.

So if cultural materialism and anthropology (including comparative studies) provide two key resources of hope of an intellectual nature, how can they be brought to bear as positive influences on the development of policy and practice in education? The additional strand that is required, and that was recognised by both Williams and Freire, is that of action, indeed political action. For both of these public intellectuals, collective action was the force that could bring about greater democracy and justice. For Williams, as a member of the British and European 'New Left', for Freire as an international activist, we saw how their involvement in social movements sought to challenge the growing influence of repressive populist elements of neoliberalism. Neither of them held much hope that mainstream political parties could do much to bring about the kinds of radical changes that were needed, either in education or in other aspects of public life. Each of them aligned themselves more closely with trade unions and with activist groupings including environmental alliances and anti-racist organisations. Now, well into the 21st century, and in the wake of 'Me Too', 'Black Lives Matter' and radical green politics, the only serious hope for the development of a more humane, democratic approach to public education must surely lie in working with and through such organisations to bring about change. We may take some inspiration from the success of Greta Thunberg and Extinction Rebellion in organising some school-based and student-led action, including school strikes.

Given the hegemonic hold that the industrial trainer lobby has gained over public education, with the promotion of phrases such as 'the knowledge economy' and 'the information age' tending to obscure the cultural and democratising elements that were so important in the historical development of education systems, current prospects for radical progressive change cannot be seen to be great. However, as I noted in my opening remarks, the potential power of collective action was realised more than once in the second half of the 20th century, so if the forces for positive change can be successfully aligned and if there is effective leadership, we can actually live in hope of education once again becoming a force for greater freedom and justice around the world.

Conclusion

Raymond Williams' acknowledgement of the wider social and political challenges, towards the conclusion of *Towards 2000*, is surely highly applicable to education around the world today:

> If there are no easy answers there are still available and discoverable hard answers, and it is these that we can now learn to make and share. This has been, from the beginning, the sense and impulse of the long revolution. (Williams, 1983, p. 269)

And this long revolution requires an underpinning of hope. Hope has never been more important, as we hear about the ongoing impact of the COVID pandemic on the mental health of young people and the dramatic increase in the number of children being taken out of school to be educated at home. The combined effects of neoliberalism, ecological disaster, destructive conflicts and the global pandemic have created a world where division and alienation are prevalent and where the power of education – ordinary education in Williams's term – must play a key part in creating hope for the future.

The great Irish poet Seamus Heaney cited one of the moving forces of democratisation in central Europe:

> Hope, according to [Vaclav] Havel, is different from optimism. It is a state of the soul rather than a response to the evidence. It is not the expectation that things will turn out successfully but the conviction that something is worth working for, however it turns out. Its deepest roots are in the transcendental, beyond the horizon.
> (from a *Sunday Tribune* article, 'Cessation, 1994', reprinted in Heaney, S. *Finders Keepers*, 2002, p. 47)

Hope may indeed have roots in the transcendental, but we also do need to develop our intellectual and political resources for hope and to deploy them carefully in a collective manner in order to bring about the sea-change that is required in society and in education in order to secure a future for those that will follow us on this planet.

References

Anderson-Levitt, K. (Ed.). (2003). *Local meanings, global schooling*. Palgrave Macmillan.

Anderson-Levitt, K. (Ed.). (2012). *Anthropologies of education*. Berghahn.

Freire, P. (1972a). *Cultural action for freedom*. Penguin.

Freire, P. (1972b). *Pedagogy of the oppressed*. Penguin.

Freire, P. (2014). *Pedagogy of hope*. Bloomsbury.

Grace, G. (1984). Urban education: Policy science or critical scholarship? In G. Grace (Ed.), *Education and the city* (pp. 3–58). Routledge & Kegan Paul.

Heaney, S. (2002). *Finders keepers*. Faber & Faber.

Menter, I. (2022). *Raymond Williams and education: History, culture, democracy*. Bloomsbury.

Menter, I. (2023). Teacher education research in the twenty-first century. In I. Menter (Ed.), *The Palgrave handbook of teacher education research* (pp. 3–32). Palgrave-Macmillan.

Williams, R. (1962). *Communications*. Penguin.

Williams, R. (1960). *Border country*. Hogarth.

Williams, R. (1961). *The long revolution*. Penguin.

THE HIDDEN LIFE OF EDUCATION

Stephen Kemmis

In *The Hidden Life of Trees*, forester Peter Wohlleben (2015/2016) described walking one morning through a familiar clearing when something caught his eye: a green-tinged beech stump that had been sawn off close to ground level many years ago. He took out his penknife and cut a slice off the outer edge of the stump. It was alive! But without a canopy of leaves and the photosynthesis necessary for the tree's growth, how could the roots of the tree still be active? What was providing it with nutrition? Years of study later, Wohlleben concluded that the stump was being kept alive by other beeches in the forest around it, through traceries of roots stretching underground from tree to tree, assisted by specialised fungi that had evolved to transfer sugars from each tree to others nearby. This vast network allowed the forest to compensate for the local conditions around each tree: differences in sunlight from one side of a hill to another; more or less favourable soil in different places; and greater or lesser competition from rival and predator species. Through this forest network, each beech contributed to sustaining the health of the forest as a whole, helping all withstand the damage caused by wind, storms, and the natural death of individual trees.

Human beings have also evolved ways of cooperating for the good of the family, the clan, the village, and the society – and also for the good for humankind and the community of life on Earth. Of course, humans are sometimes also difficult, quarrelsome, and violent, but mostly they cooperate for the common good.

People come to cooperate partly through *socialisation* – a more or less invisible process by which people are initiated into the everyday practices of their communities, by which they learn *how to go on* (Wittgenstein, 1953/1958) in their families and communities. When the process is deliberately arranged to initiate others into especially valued practices, however, we call it *education*, that is, when it is consciously organised with the double purpose of forming persons and worlds (Kemmis, 2023).

Through education, children, young people, and adults are initiated into

a. *forms of understanding* that enlarge learners' faculties of individual and collective *self-expression*;
b. *modes of action* that enhance learners' capacities for individual and collective *self-development*; and
c. *ways of relating to one another and the world* that foster learners' powers of individual and collective *self-determination*,

with the aims of attaining the good for each person, the good for humankind, and the good for the community of life on Earth. When people – not just educators – act educationally, they aim to develop learners'

a. faculties of self-expression, not only so they can think and speak clearly but also to help secure *a culture based on reason*;
b. capacities for self-development, not just for the sake of their own productivity and survival, but also to help secure *productive and sustainable economies and environments*; and
c. powers of self-determination, not just for the sake of their own autonomy and responsibility, but also to help secure *just and democratic communities and societies*.

Education should not be confused with *schooling*. The philosopher Alastair MacIntyre (1983) described the dialectical relationship of mutual constitution that exists between *practices* and *institutions*. An example is the dialectical relationship between the practice of *education* and the institutions of *schooling*. But MacIntyre also notes that the relationship between practices and institutions is bedevilled with tensions and contradictions.

MacIntyre defines practices as cooperatively developed forms of human activity conducted in the pursuit of the distinctive 'internal goods' of each practice – like the goods of attaining health through the practice of medicine. On the other hand, he says, the internal goods of a practice (attaining health) are always made vulnerable by the very institutions (like hospitals) that were created to nurture the relevant practices. The tensions and contradictions between practices and institutions arise because, if they are to survive, institutions are necessarily caught up in the pursuit of 'external goods' like money, power, and status. Pursuing these external goods can endanger the pursuit of the internal goods of a practice. In recent decades, for instance, we have seen what happens when institutions like universities become so preoccupied with their budgets and various kinds of 'outcomes' that they are diverted from their care for the practices of education, research, and community engagement. When this happens, they put at risk the conditions necessary for nurturing the practices of teaching and learning and research, and nurturing the people involved – teachers and learners and researchers.

Under contemporary pressures of funding and neoliberal surveillance and accountability, education institutions at every level have come under increased strain. All experience the tensions, contradictions, and contestation of sustaining excellence in the *practices* of education under conditions of diminished funding and more intense external scrutiny of the extent to which education *institutions* achieve the officially-approved 'outcomes' against which their performance is measured. In the case of universities, for example, such outcomes include measures of student access, retention, and success; and quantity and quality of research publications and research income. Various measures of 'impact' and 'quality' have been manufactured to compare universities internationally, in league tables like the *Times Higher Education World University Rankings*, the *US News Global University Rankings*, or the *Shanghai Academic Ranking of World Universities*.

Nevertheless, despite the pressures of diminished funding and surveillance, teachers teach, and students learn, often in ingenious, exciting, engaging, and generative ways. Despite the corrosive pressures, excellent education continues and persists in many education institutions. But in Australian universities, for example, many teachers and researchers report that life and work is increasingly difficult and challenging. Morale is crashing. More academics contemplate leaving the profession – and do. Fewer students enter courses preparing them for work in the education profession, and fewer graduate. Fewer students choose to study teacher education.

In everyday life, as well as in education institutions, teachers and learners continue to form communities of practice in which learners are socialised to

a. speak the language and specialist discourses of their fields (enlarging their forms of understanding and their faculties of self-expression);

b. engage in the specialist 'ways we do things around here' – ways of working in their field (enhancing their modes of action and their capacities for self-development); and

c. relate to others and the world in ways familiar in the communities of practice of their fields (extending their ways of relating to others and the world, and their powers of self-determination).

As they become 'old hands' in different communities of practice, learners learn 'how to go on' and 'how to fit in', whether in a day-care centre for infants, a primary school, a university seminar, or in work experience, or an apprenticeship in a workplace. Just because they are in education institutions, however, it does not mean that learners are being *educated*. Generally, they are being socialised into the ways of being of their communities. Sometimes, however, they are being *trained* into unreflectively applying skills they are mastering or even being *indoctrinated* into officially-approved ways of thinking, doing things, and relating to others and the world. Nevertheless, on many occasions, newcomers are not just being *socialised* into communities of practice but also *educated* – when their socialisation is enriched by the double purpose of education: the aims of helping people to live well in worlds worth living in. People sometimes overlook this kind of *socialisation-education* in communities of practice because it happens in 'hidden' ways – concealed, like the underground transfer of nutrients between the trees in the beech forest.

Traditionally, we think of education institutions as specialised places where *knowledge* is transferred from one person to another, and from one generation to another. I beg to differ. I think it is not so much *knowledge* being transferred as *practices* being *shared*. While people coming to education institutions are frequently fixated on learning or teaching 'knowledge', what happens in fact is a sharing of the kinds of *practices* characteristic of different kinds of local and professional communities of practices. Yes, the student learns (a) the languages and discourses and symbols of a field, but the field is composed of practices, not only knowledge. Learners learn *how to go on* in the languages, discourses, and symbols that make the field comprehensible to people who practise in it, and that allows them to communicate with one another. At the same time, they learn (b) how to go on in the ways of doing and producing things (whether debating, or constructing, or analysing, or healing) in that field, using the spaces, materials, resources, facilities, equipment, tools, and times relevant in doing the work. Those activities and that work is what the field is *for*. And, along with those things, they learn (c) how to go on in the ways of relating to others and to the world that are appropriate in that field – for example, recognising and relating to clients, customers, colleagues, students, patients … They learn appropriate ways of connecting, appropriate ways of feeling, and appropriate ways of contributing to people and the world, despite the conflict, opposition, resistance, and contestation that may happen along the way. By learning these things, newcomers become old hands, novices become experts, and rising generations become custodians of the communities of practices that support the multiple, differentiated kinds of life and work and occupations of their professions, disciplines, communities, nations, and the world.

When teachers and education institutions mechanically push students through the curriculum, however, or slavishly follow the routines and rituals of approved pedagogies, or administer only the approved assessments, their efforts may not be educational. If they are not stimulating individual and collective self-expression, self-development, and self-determination, and if they are not aiming their efforts both at the good for each learner and the good for humankind and the community of life on Earth, their efforts may simply be *non-educational* or even *anti-educational*. They may be engaging in nothing more than a kind of official *training* (in the sense of the unreflective reproduction of skills) or *indoctrination* of learners into officially approved ways of thinking, doing things, and relating to others and the world.

In everyday life, people are always learning. They learn whether or not they are engaging with and being challenged and changed by what a teacher is teaching. In my view, *people can't help learning*. They learn all the time when they are engaged in *any* practice. They are always ready to vary what they do in response to changing needs or circumstances, ready to mimic or imitate (openly or in thought) what someone demonstrates, ready to join relevant conversations, activities, and relationships. Teachers intend and hope such things will happen for their students, but the students may be learning things other than those their teachers intend. In my view, learning is 'coming to practise differently' (Kemmis, 2021). It is what Lave and Packer (2008, p. 44) call a process of 'ontological transformation' – a process of becoming through which people change their identities, their ways of being, and through which they change the world around them. To put it provocatively, learning happens whenever people practise, always and everywhere.

As Lave (2019) points out, learning is always situated – situated in practice settings that support different kinds of communities of practice. Learning happens in supermarkets, apprenticeships, watching football games, dancing the Tango, and in schools. In everyday life, it is as 'natural' as breathing. It is what human beings (and many other species) do. It is socialisation that doesn't only *reproduce* the ways of doing things that have gone before but also varies, adapts, and *transforms* those ways of doing things.

Education also happens in 'hidden' ways, even when it happens in plain sight in the classroom or seminar or lecture hall. We see the lecturer lecturing, the teacher teaching, the master guiding the apprentice. We may believe that it is teachers who make education happen. When things are going well, teachers are teaching *and*, because of or despite their efforts, students *learn*. But education – not just learning – also goes on in everyday life. We see education going on in education institutions when we view them front-on, but, seen from the back, we see socialisation – socialisation into the forms of life of communities of practice, whether in the classroom, in the institution, in a profession, or in a workplace. Socialisation happens whenever people adjust their practising in changing circumstances. It happens through the hidden web of human sociality – a web like the concealed tracery of connections between the roots of the trees in the beech forest.

Often, but not always, socialisation turns out also to be education. Education initiates people into practices in which one person (or several) helps others to speak and think well, to act well in the world, and to relate well to others and the community of life on the planet. Not all processes of socialisation have these guiding lights, but, on those occasions when people do act deliberately for the best, socialisation is frequently also education. Thus, the plumber or electrician who shows an apprentice how to do a good job may not only be socialising the apprentice to ways of doing things, but also educating them into a way of being a certain – *professional* – kind of plumber or electrician. The leading second violinist who helps the new second violinist to become a voice within the combined voice of the orchestra might likewise be not just socialising but also educating them. And parents and families educate children when they show them not only how to behave or what to do in a particular situation but also help them to understand and experience why this is a *good* way to do things in the world.

This *education-socialisation* goes on unremarked and unheralded in everyday life, as another form of people's initiation into practices, when socialisation is accompanied by an awareness of a larger purpose – when learners come to know and experience how particular skills or capabilities fit into life, and into lives worth living. Often, a colleague, companion, guide, or mentor brings out this sense of a wider purpose. Often, people also do it for them-selves, self-reflectively, through critical consideration of the nature and con-sequences of their actions.

Sometimes, however, institutions apparently devoted to education become so narrowly focussed on the transmission of knowledge, skills, and values that their efforts turn out to be only socialisation, or unreflective skills training, or indoctrination. In Australia today, this is increasingly common. Many teachers, from early childhood education to universities, experience the *deprofessionalisation* of their work as a source of real and demoralising tension. They complain that they feel they are perceived as mere operatives – cogs in the wheels – of imperious education systems.

The surveillance teachers experience at the hands of neoliberal account-ability systems has become so intense that they find it harder – sometimes much harder – to make time and space for the greater educational purpose of helping learners to live well in worlds worth living in. Despite their com-mitment to listening to the voices of the learners in front of them, they are increasingly obliged to obey the orders their managers whisper insidiously over their shoulders. Education is *denatured* by those accountability pressures. They subjugate the purposes of education to strident official demands that schooling be no more than mimicry, training, or indoctrination.

Still, education goes on despite these tough times. Some of it happens on the margins in institutions, some happens outside educational institutions. It may be unremarked, because it is unremarkable: it happens at all sorts of times in everyday life. But people always know it's happening when they are part of it. In everyday life, it is hidden in plain sight, in the ubiquitous double process of forming persons and societies.

Education doesn't stand still. It realises shared *hopes* for people and the world: shared hopes that it can serve the individual and collective interests of everyone it touches, including students, teachers, parents and caregivers, school and system leaders, and whole communities and societies. Current forms of education have evolved to meet the changing historical circum-stances of different cultures, economies, environments, and societies, and educators work hard to find appropriate forms through which contemporary education can meet new and emerging circumstances. The task is not the exclusive preserve of professional educators, however. Plenty of others grap-ple with it too: mentors, coaches, guides, colleagues, parents, friends, peers, helpers … And it takes *courage* to find new forms for education – new forms of educational practice that will in fact help people to live well in worlds worth living in. It takes courage to resist easy and superficial solutions, and to resist the siren calls and insidious whisperings of administrators preoccupied by administrative and financial systems management; to resist the entreaties of those who offer only administrative responses to educational problems, who think that education is the administration of teachers and learners.

The courage needed is not a kind of bravado. It comes from a *wisdom* grounded in deep historical understanding and open-minded, open-eyed, critical analysis of contemporary circumstances. This kind of wisdom arises from, recalls, represents, anticipates, and returns to its use in *practice*, to its life in *history*. It is driven by the desire to make a concrete, *practical* difference in people's everyday lives and the lives of their communities.

The world needs educators with the wisdom and courage to turn hope into new realities – to realise new and better worlds, worlds worth living in (Kemmis, 2023). And these new worlds need a new generation of educators willing to take their turn as the stewards of education for their times and places: people who can interpret the world through the lens of education – people knowledgeable about and grounded in traditions of educational practice who can step up and take their turn to transform education *in practice* and *in history* for new and emerging times.

To ask for such people is not to ask for heroes. It is to ask for people who know what education is, and what it is for. It is to ask for *educators* – people who *know how to go on* in education, in practice, in the history that is always unfolding in the eternal present, trailing the consequences from which wise practitioners learn. It is to ask for people who speak the distinctive language and discourses of education, do the distinctive work and activities of education, and inhabit distinctively educational ways of relating to others and the world. MacIntyre (1983) described people educated in the histories and practical traditions and ways of working of their professions as people who live *a certain kind of life*. The world today needs educators who know how to live the certain kind of life that is educating. Not just teaching or socialising or training or indoctrinating. The world needs educators who can initiate rising generations of teachers into the historically-formed, historically-changing practice of education.

This is to say emphatically that the world does *not* need teacher educators that can do no more than teach the official curriculum using officially-approved forms of pedagogy, and to use approved forms of evaluation and assessment to determine whether learners have learned the content ('learning outcomes') of the official curriculum. Australia is awash with official curriculum, pedagogies, and assessments, however. They are prescribed by authorities including the Australian Curriculum and Assessment Authority (ACARA, established 2008) to oversee national curriculum initiatives and assessments; the Australian Institute for Teaching and School Leadership (AITSL, established 2010), to oversee standards for the teaching profession and for school leaders; and the Australian Education Ministers Meeting (Ministers of Education from the Commonwealth and the States and Territories; which succeeded the Education Council, established 2014, which succeeded meetings of Education Ministers under the aegis of the Council of Australian Governments, COAG). Fearing that Australia will slip behind in international rankings of school achievement, these organisations have prescribed national curricula, professional standards and pedagogies, and assessments. By doing so, they have imposed what they believe will be educational on education institutions across the country. And yet, by doing so, they have deprofessionalised education. They have usurped the educational prerogatives of educators, starved them of the oxygen of critical reflection on their own professional educational practice, and turned them into the operatives of national systems of schooling.

Despite the official prescriptions, and the intrusive management and monitoring, most teachers continue to reflect thoughtfully and critically on the nature and consequences of their educational practice, and adjust their practice to meet the needs and opportunities of changing times and circumstances. They do, in fact, learn from their practice. And, when they are well-informed about the history and traditions of their profession, they participate consciously and deliberately in the processes by which educational practices and traditions evolve. In doing so, they may find themselves at odds with officially-approved curriculum content, pedagogies, and assessments. At such moments, they are faced with a choice: whether to intervene in the interests of *these* learners, *this* community, and *this* education profession, or obediently follow the officially-approved curriculum, pedagogies, and assessments. And this is what calls for wisdom and the courage to act in the interests of the learners in front of them, and the local and professional communities in which they live and work, rather than meekly to follow orders.

And so, today, many teachers do their most important educational work, both in classrooms and in the communities of practice that constitute the profession, at the margins of the official curriculum, pedagogies, and assessments, out of the glare of the managed and monitored theatre of schooling.

Education thrives today in the littoral zone beyond the sand and rock of officialdom; it reaches out into the ocean of life.

This littoral zone is where today's educational practice changes and evolves to meet the new and emerging realities of the contemporary world. Education systems may have colonised much of the time and space of schooling with curricula, pedagogies and assessments that alienate learners and learning, and oblige teachers to spend time motivating unmotivated learners to learn. But in the communities of practice in classrooms, workplaces, and communities, socialisation-education continues, and teachers and students engage in education for living well and for creating worlds worth living in.

The task for the teachers of today and tomorrow is to find and inhabit that littoral zone, to participate in its hidden life of education, helping learners to explore and navigate it. Then, as experienced guides to this hidden life, they can fulfil their collective professional obligation to renew education for changing times and circumstances.

References

Kemmis, S. (2021). A practice theory perspective on learning: Beyond a 'standard' view. *Studies in Continuing Education, 43*(3), 280–295. https://doi.org/10.1080/0158037X.2021.1920384

Kemmis, S. (2023). Education for living well in a world worth living in. In K. E. Reimer, M. Kaukko, S. Windsor, K. Mahon, & S. Kemmis (Eds.), *Living well in a world worth living in for all: Vol. 1: Current practices of social justice, sustainability and wellbeing* (pp. 13–25). Springer.

Lave, J., & Packer, M. (2008). Towards a social ontology of learning. In K. Nielsen, S. Brinkmann, C. Elmholdt, L. Tanggard, P. Musaeus, & G. Kraft (Eds.), *A qualitative stance: In memory of Steinar Kvale, 1938–2008* (pp. 17–46). Aarhus Universitetsforlag.

Lave, J. (2019). *Learning in everyday life: Access, participation, and changing practice.* Cambridge University Press.

MacIntyre, A. (1983). *After virtue: A study in moral theory* (2nd ed.) Duckworth.

Wittgenstein, L. (1953/1958). *Philosophical investigations* (3rd ed.) (G.E.M. Anscombe, Trans.). Basil Blackwell & Mott Ltd.

Wohlleben, P. (2015/2016). *The hidden life of trees: What they feel, how they communicate* (J. Billinghurst, Trans.). Black Inc. (originally published by Ludwig Verlag.)

HOPE, EDUCATION AND THE GENERATION OF FEAR: MATTERS OF TIME AND SPACE

Catherine Burke

> Hope is not happiness or confidence or inner peace; it's a commitment to search for possibilities. (Solnit, The Guardian, 27/07/23)

Hope in education is the courage to search for and realise possibilities in past and present practice to expand our imagination of what school can be. Schooling is peculiarly resistant to change but as presently constituted, the form of education provided regularly fails large numbers of the school population, creates distress and, according to many employers, is unfit for the 21st century. The history of education is peppered with crises as well as radical experiments and more sustained administrative endeavours to bring about change. This is often referred to as the pendulum effect where there is a constant movement between the avocation of progressive and more traditional methods. In England, the national crisis brought about by the last world war stimulated a commitment to invest in education through wide scale building programmes and initiatives to strengthen democracy. For young children, this ultimately meant being encouraged, either by means of the design of the building or the curriculum to use time and space differently. There were expectations that young children would spend less time in their seats, more time on their feet, constructing and experimenting and expressing themselves through language, music, art and movement. For teachers this meant a challenge to conventional teaching practices. Ample courage was required to change ways of working supported by an empathetic inspection regime. In the more progressive regions of the country, teachers were encouraged to visit schools in other places, sometimes in the locality, occasionally in another country, to observe directly and learn what was considered to be best practice. In the immediate decades following the war, this combination of crisis, institutional support for teachers and attention to matters of time and space created a 'revolution' in primary education that attracted visitors from across the world. Hope was created out of such exchanges and teaching was, for a while at least, liberated; teachers were proud of their work and profession. This success was at first celebrated as many educationalists came to see for themselves and document in books and films what was happening in the English primary school.[1] During the 1970s, a concerted effort by traditionalists eager to reassert control over the profession to undermine this progress led to the gradual erosion of hope. Their efforts succeeded by encouraging fear among parents and the wider communities; fear of progressive teachers and their methods.

Writing about the survival of modern day capitalism, the late anthropologist, David Graeber, argued 'hopelessness isn't natural. It needs to be produced' The primary task of our institutions, he suggested, is to create and maintain *hopelessness through the production of fear*. This fear, he argues, needs to be reproduced anew for every generation. Graeber asks, is it normal for human beings to be unable to imagine a better world? We might want to ask, is it normal for us to be unable to imagine a better world through education?

Since the start of the millennium, a slow revolution in teaching and learning has taken place. For decades it has been possible to access the curriculum successfully outside of the classroom. Access to the Internet at home, slow at first, has become ever more available yet school-based pedagogy has proven to be immune to the transformation in possibilities implied. The school and the classroom have remained largely unaltered. It took another crisis to change expectations and stimulate alternative possibilities.

The Covid-19 pandemic brought about a public health crisis across the world and serious disruption to schooling resulted in a range of changes to everyday experience. In the United Kingdom, this disruption altered key relationships of schooling: relationships between pupils and their peers; between teachers and pupils; between schools and community. In schools that remained open for the children of key workers, relationships between bodies and space became altered. With fewer pupils in attendance, in many instances more than usual amounts of space and time became available, allowing for imaginative and creative approaches to learning through play, making, and modelling. For a time at least, the school building ceased to be the primary and singular site of learning. Many schools closed their doors completely. It did not take long for politicians to begin lamenting what they termed 'learning loss'; measured quantities of lost learning they estimated to be occurring. They even calculated precise future loss of earnings for the cohorts of pupils affected by the pandemic. There was seldom any other line of thought; no acknowledgement that for some children an escape from the classroom might have, for a period, enhanced their experience of learning and sense of well-being. Scant regard was paid to any notion of the present organisation of teaching and learning in schools being unfit for purpose, leading many pupils to fail to thrive and many teachers to leave the profession. Politicians, preferring to peddle fear, paid very little attention to the positive aspects of these changes but where they happened, parents took note. Matters of space were brought seriously into question as sites of learning became expanded, incorporating teenagers' bedrooms and homes more generally. Outdoors offered relatively safe spaces for education and in some places pop-up structures appeared in schoolyards providing basic airy shelter at least in the summer months. Elsewhere, school spilled into village halls, community centres and other public assets in the locality. Almost overnight, the school without walls envisaged by John Dewey, Ivan Illich, Colin Ward and a range of lesser-known progressive head teachers over the 20th century began to be realised. At the time, the prevailing narrative was one of fearful, profound and lasting damage. This narrative continues post-pandemic taking the form of a lamentation for a lost generation of youngsters, many of whom have continued to remain absent from school.

In the United Kingdom and in several other countries, school attendance has fallen significantly. In England, this is being described as a 'national crisis' and coincides with a breakdown of trust in the school inspection regime after the tragic death, through suicide, of a primary school head teacher whose school had been formally declared 'inadequate' by the inspectorate. Many parents, having lived through changes to work practices during the pandemic, have recalculated the benefits or otherwise of school attendance five days a week. Unprecedented numbers of parents are voting with their feet. A window has opened into the grim reality, for many pupils and their teachers, of target driven instruction, informal testing regimes, autocratic disciplinary measures and public examinations. Many children experience deep levels of anxiety and distress simply by attending school and the failure to provide adequate and suitable education and care for all, regardless of abilities, compounds the situation. This 'window' has revealed a vast landscape of vulnerability and those responsible for designing the parameters of education are now struggling to close it. The default position is to cite the pandemic as the key cause of disengagement with school. Few, if any, cite the curriculum, pedagogy and disciplinary regimes that have increasingly served to dampen potential curiosity and excitement and are responsible for so much distress. The reaction of political bodies responsible for schooling is the further generation of fear. Talk of a 'lost generation' peppers the predominantly negative narrative of fear and failure; the supposed failure of poor parenting and the fear of social disapproval backed up by fines.

Hopelessness through the production of fear

Considering Graeber's proposition with regard to the design of modern schooling leads us to uncomfortable territory. We recoil at the notion of fear in the context of our intention to educate. But the generation of fear is essential to the project of school as we know it by means of generating a degree of hopelessness in assessing the possibilities of radical change. Arguably, the survival of modern day schooling relies on the generation of fear within and beyond the classroom. The antithesis of fear is courage and the process of shifting from a position of fear to one of courage is what we might identify as hope.

So how is it possible for this courage to emerge? Schooling relies upon a set of assumptions first established by the industrial economies in the late 19th and early 20th centuries. These assumptions or 'truths' about the contours of education break into relief at times of crisis revealing their vulnerabilities, stimulating a response designed to recover and shore them up. The crisis in schooling brought about by the global pandemic disturbed, for a while, the material and temporal conditions for learning and teaching and in so doing, possible futures came to be experienced in the present. The predominantly negative narrative of 'learning loss' has produced a degree of fear and moral panic. However, this has so far failed to convince large numbers of a somewhat more critically aware public of the necessity of everyday school attendance and has disturbed the general acceptance that school time should roughly mirror work time.

An alternative reading of the impact of lockdowns and school closures is possible; one that suggests the pandemic has created useful and hope-filled ruptures in prevailing mythologies of education.

During one of the several periods of lockdown, I began to consider what general assumptions effectively fuelled this acute sense of danger. For purposes of brevity and to help me think about relationships of time, space and place, I drew together what I considered to be ten mythologies of education. They were intended to provoke discussion and were posted on various social media sites.

Ten mythologies of education

1. That children learn best in buildings set apart from the community called schools.
2. That there is a predicted scale against which children's development may accurately be measured.
3. That learning takes place best in spaces called classrooms among peers of the same age.
4. That knowledge is best acquired through instruction.
5. That what is measurable matters most in education.
6. That children's mental health is always best secured by attending school.
7. That school time should roughly mirror work time
8. That there is a common pace in which to learn and that slowing down a bit threatens educational progress.
9. That models of progressive schooling in the past that emphasised curiosity, an arts-led curriculum and discovery learning are not appropriate for today.
10. That we all agree and know what education is and what it is for.[2]

Popularly held beliefs about education abound and operate powerfully in the realm of 'common sense' passed on from generation to generation. They act as closed boxes, held together by fear, containing assumptions that are ubiquitous and seemingly unquestionable. As such they not only constrain the possibilities of teaching and learning but they limit the parameters of research. Often concerned with aspects of time and space, adherence to them holds key elements of schooling in place. It is notable how many of these statements have been challenged by progressive experiments in education in the past. Similarly, in the contemporary context there are examples of practice pushing at the boundaries of these positions characterised by alterations in relationships between time and space.

A primary myth that underpins this dominant narrative is that children learn best in buildings set apart from the community called schools. And that learning takes place best in spaces called classrooms among peers of the same age. Both of these contentions have been challenged time and again over the past century by progressive educationalists in Europe, Australasia and the United States . The places where learning happens have at times been expanded in the educational imagination. Since the emergence of computer based teaching and learning in the late 1990s it has been increasingly possible for the school curriculum to be accessed beyond the school walls. Why this has failed to happen, to any large degree, has been remarked on as well as the tendency of traditional forms of teaching and learning to be so resistant to change. This goes a long way to explain the failure of online learning that was put in place during the school closures. Teachers were ill equipped to exploit the possibilities available to them in computer-based learning. Nevertheless, the pandemic allowed the certainty of key mythologies of education to be shaken at least temporarily and expanded the imagined spaces and places of learning.

The experience of learning and teaching outside of the school walls could be said to have created a rupture in the collective expectation of what a school could or should be. Lost time and abandoned spaces characterised the period of Covid lockdowns across the world and new spatial relationships underpinning the experience of education were brought into focus. The very definition of school space was expanded through the real experience of teachers and pupils in schools and that of parents and their children at home. For a while it became possible to imagine education being supported through and within a far greater variety of settings than is the usual case and the fundamental and basic requirement for care and nurture, whether in the school or in the home, was shown to be pivotal.

Amongst the many surveys assessing parental attitudes during the periods of lockdown, one carried out in the spring of 2021 by the United Kingdom's Institute of Fiscal Studies reported that two-thirds of those parents surveyed were concerned about the amount of learning lost. This was not surprising given the insistent negative narrative at the time. However, the same survey found that 83% of respondents were in favour of policies to promote children's wellbeing. Most believed that increasing time spent learning through the arts, creative writing and accessing learning outside of the classroom would make the biggest difference to learning recovery.[3] Around the same time, a survey of German parents revealed predictable concern about learning loss but also significant numbers reporting improved emotional stability in children who were unable to attend school. These comments reflect the emergence of hopeful possibilities drawn from the experience of changes that at least temporarily disturbed the prevailing notions of what a school should be.

In the United Kingdom widespread social and economic fear was, and continues to be, generated by means of rhetoric of 'learning loss', 'falling behind' and need for 'catching-up'. Post pandemic, the generation of fear presents us with the notion of a 'lost generation'. Underpinning this emotionally laden language is a reservoir of fear maintained by reference to images of schooling designed to reassure. For example, during the first lockdown, the then secretary of state for education in the United Kingdom declared that when pupils returned to schools their desks should be arranged in rows. That any other arrangement of bodies in school spaces should occur would seem to threaten the social contract between parents and schools.

Resistance to schooling

In the United Kingdom, it is assessed that the number of children persistently absent from school has doubled since before the pandemic. In 2017/18, 11.7% of pupils missed 10 or more sessions (defined as half a day of school); in 2021/22, 23.5% of pupils missed 10 or more sessions.[4] Not confined to the United Kingdom, the United States has reported a doubling of school absenteeism since before the pandemic.

Continuing the negative narrative of learning loss and fear, this matter is discussed in terms of massive and permanent individual, social and economic damage. A dominant argument points to the rise in reported incidences of ill health, particularly mental ill health as a root cause. Disaffection and school refusal sometimes gets a mention as does dysfunctional family life. Rarely is there mention of children and their parents or guardians taking decisions to limit school attendance having experienced positive outcomes of home based learning. Significantly, it has been reported that some parents had realised through the periods of school closures that their offspring had experienced improved motivation and increased mental well-being. A Centre for Social Justice think tank survey reported that 28% of UK parents consulted agreed that 'the pandemic has shown it is not essential for children to attend school every day'.

There is evidence that absenteeism is widespread and not only strongly associated with poverty and deprivation. There are signs that disaffection with school among parents and pupils is due to the inability of schools as presently constituted to provide an attractive personalised experience of education. British children and young people regularly are recorded as amongst the most stressed and unhappy in international surveys. This is not a new situation caused by the pandemic, but a chronic systemic feature of the experience of schooling over decades. Government and major political parties offer a limited range of solutions, few of which recognise the elephant in the room: the curriculum. The marketisation of schooling has produced its own Frankenstein and the one-size-fits-all curriculum is widely felt to be lacking in humanity. In these conditions a renewed contract between teachers, pupils and community appears to be urgent. However, the greatest need is to engage all stakeholders in seriously debating the question of what education should look like and how it should be experienced in the 21st century.

Children and young people have time and again clearly expressed what matters to them in helping them to learn and thrive. Surveys such as 'The school I'd like' in the United Kingdom (2001 and 2011) and a similar survey in Australia (2005) revealed the rich capacity of school pupils and others (home educated, hospitalised, traveller children) to address the fundamental assumptions about what a school should be and the place and pace of learning. Their imaginations of possibilities envisaged school as an inclusive place which contained everything, rather like a city. Learning would happen through active engagement with real world issues where solutions to problems were currently urgent. Young people's active engagement with the climate emergency is a clear indication of this. It should, one said, be no longer acceptable to expect children to write essays on topics without engaging in the real world fully. In School I'd Like surveys youngsters wanted time to think and time enough to finish a piece of work. They wanted comfortable domestic spaces to learn, work and play in. Teachers were important, but so were other members of the community who could share their knowledge.[5] In fact their responses can be seen to touch on most of my ten suggested mythologies of education.

Slowing down a bit

Time shapes every aspect of schooling: From the setting of the timetable to the frequency of playtime; from the division of the school day into chunks of time in class and 'on task' to the rhythms of the school year. Then there is wasted time where tasks are set that fail to stimulate the interest of pupils leading to disruption and disaffection or where insufficient time is allotted to activities leading to frustration and noncompliance. The language of 'catch up' and 'falling behind' assumes an expected and predictable pace of learning. Engendering a sense of permanent damage to a 'lost generation' relies on assumptions about the essential parameters of learning and the pace in which it occurs. 'Slow pedagogy' challenges the notion that there is a common pace in which to learn and that slowing down a bit threatens educational progress. In her book, *Slow Learning and the Unhurried Child*, (2022) Alison Clark makes the case for possibilities of deeper engagement and improved well-being in young children by paying attention to matters of time and pace. This important book focussing on the early years also provides a rich exemplar of possibilities for older children who have so often voiced their frustrations in not having sufficient time to complete their learning or not having time to follow through with questions and curiosities that arise from school work. The argument is not to reduce all activities to a slow pace but to pay attention to how expectations of pace can be varied and ample time given to support reflection and critical engagement with new knowledge.

Slow pedagogy offers hope across the whole spectrum of learning dispositions as it recognises and takes seriously human variation in the time it takes for individuals to absorb and process information. It recognises the function of reflection and the importance of allowing time to complete tasks satisfactorily. It is particularly relevant to the neurodivergent for whom existing structures of schooling so often fail. Adopting the principles and practices of slow pedagogy obviously challenges the whole regime of testing and target setting but its benefits, especially for pupils' mental health may prove of greater value.

'There is a crack in everything. That's how the light gets in.' (Leonard Cohen)

'To hope is dangerous and yet it is the opposite of fear'[6] Rebecca Solnit articulates a truth that it takes courage to pursue a form of education that works for all. Imagination is critical to the task, as is commitment to honestly question the taken for granted in education. It has been thought for many decades that schools would morph into very different kinds of places where they would act as hubs for processing information and knowledge acquired outside of the classroom through active engagement in real-world activities. There has been a confidence that the classroom itself would disappear as it came to be found unsuitable to the expanded varieties of learning experience envisaged. School itself would expand into the community and embrace learners of all ages. Teachers would become equipped with expert subject knowledge but also research practitioners able to pass on their skills to pupils in their care. All of this is relevant to the present state of affairs where there is an emerging awareness that other possibilities, beyond the classroom, exist.

It is nowhere near enough to provide schools with mentors and counsellors to address the appalling rise in cases of mental ill health. High levels of distress were apparent long before the Covid pandemic. The pandemic caused a rupture in the fabric of schooling, a breach that allows for a root and branch reappraisal of the expectations of contemporary schooling. We can hope and we can dream, like 14-year-old Maisie from London:

> I dream of happiness and learning united. I dream of no interruptions
> If I went to my ideal school I wouldn't wake up every morning and dread the next day, the next week, the next year, and the rest of my life.[7]

Notes

1 Burke C., Cunningham, P. and Hoare, L. (2021) *Education through the arts for well-being and the community: The vision and legacy of Sir Alec Clegg*. Routledge. London
2 https://architectureandeducation.org/2020/07/01/mythologies-of-education-in-the-time-of-covid-19/
3 Covid: Parents worry about lost learning as schools reopen. March 7th 2021. https://www.bbc.co.uk/news/education-56292525
4 Source L.S.E. https://blogs.lse.ac.uk/politicsandpolicy/the-rising-tide-of-school-absences-in-the-post-pandemic-era/
5 For a full report see Catherine Burke and Ian Grosvenor (2003) *The School I'd Like. Children's and Young People's Reflections on an Education for the 21st century'* London. Routledge
6 Rebecca Solnit (2016) *Hope in the Dark*. Edinburgh: Canongate Books.
7 Burke and Grosvenor, (2003) p. 133

PEDAGOGICAL POSSIBILITIES IN AND BEYOND CLIMATE-CHANGING CLASSROOMS

Eve Mayes, with Natasha Abhayawickrama and Emma Heyink

Deakin University

Then

2008: It is another stubbornly hot and humid afternoon in my top floor English classroom in south-west Sydney. I usher a tangled group of Year 8 students from outside the classroom, down the stairs of E-block, across the baking concrete playground, up the stairs of B-block, to one of two classrooms at the school with an audio projector and a large canvas screen. We are going to watch the documentary *An Inconvenient Truth* (2006) (Guggenheim, 2006) – about former US Vice President Al Gore's campaign to 'awaken' people to the 'planetary emergency' of (what was called at the time) 'global warming'.

In one scene of the documentary, Al Gore speaks to a studio audience, standing next to a five-meter high and ten-meter wide digital graph of 60,000 years of carbon dioxide and temperature. Al Gore moves to stand on a moving cherry-picker platform, as the platform ascends upwards to a point that marks 'today's CO2 concentration' – dramatically higher than the 'natural cycle'. He continues, 'when some of these children who are here are my age, here's what it's going to be – in less than 50 years.'

The audience chuckles with the sound of the ascending cherry-picker as the platform and the red line soars upwards exponentially to a new point: 'Projected concentration after 50 more years of unrestricted fossil fuel burning'. Gore dryly observes, 'you've heard of off the charts' and there are further laughs from the studio audience.

In this classroom in 2008, I vaguely remember students tittering at the tragicomedy of Al Gore clunkily lurching upwards on the noisy platform. Amidst these amused reactions to Al Gore's slapstick upward propulsion, a student shouted out in indignation that more hadn't been done to stem the tide of rising emissions.

The key concept that I had written in the unit plan for this Year 8 Documentary study of *An Inconvenient Truth* was: '*Students can take action in the world. A critical approach to texts and to the world is empowering.*'

I can't recall what I hoped would happen when watching this documentary: what kind of 'action' I hoped students might be inspired to take: writing a letter to a local politician; taking individual action to reduce their own carbon footprint; joining a climate action group. I can't recall if and how students said they felt about this documentary; I have no idea what they felt when they went home that night (if anything): perhaps a heady cocktail of despair, anxiety, hope and paralysis? I am not so sure if these students found these pedagogical experiences to be 'empowering', as I'd written in the unit plan.

In this documentary, Gore appears to believe in the power of hearing 'the facts' to drive political and socio-ecological change. I think, at the time, I might have felt the same.

Now

2024: I have spent the last six years talking and co-researching with young people about climate change, young people's climate justice activism, and schooling. The students who were in my Year 8 class in 2008 may well now have their own children; the young people that I have recently been speaking with may not even have been born when *An Inconvenient Truth* was released. They all are, as we all are, now living in the exponential curve that Gore's audience marvelled at, with cascading climate impacts across the planet.

My turn to research with young people involved in climate activism outside of school came with the mass eruption of youth-led climate action from 2018 onwards, associated with Greta Thunberg and the Fridays For Future movement (known in Australia as School Strike 4 Climate). In 2018, the critical pedagogue in me was elated to see these mass mobilisations of young people, who collectively refused the political and pedagogical status quo, demanding bold and transformative action to address the climate crisis and build a more just and sustainable future for all. In Australia, students held up placards and banners painted with slogans including: 'Activism is learning' and 'We're missing our lessons so we can teach you one'.

But it seemed that there was more at work in these mass embodied demonstrations of climate activism, outside schooling spaces but within school-time, than lots of students who had watched climate-related documentaries in school classrooms. These mass mobilisations did not necessarily seem to have sprung from what students had learned at school – or teachers 'empowering' them. Blanche Verlie has decribed the school strikes as 'collectives' emerging 'through practices of making ecological distress explicit and public, and thus using it as a source of communal motivation and strength' (2022, p. 13). I have been curious, since the explosion of these strikes in 2018 and 2019, about the resonances and differences between the content and pedagogies at work in these out-of-school collective gatherings and school classrooms, and what an education worthy of the present might look, sound and feel like.

Pedagogical possibilities

In the research conversations that I've recently been part of in recent years, our research team has invited young people involved in climate justice activism to tell the story of how they became concerned about climate change, taking action, and climate justice. I've been curious to listen to the stories of the experiences students have had, while at school, learning about climate change, and to the differences between students' learning experiences across embodied identities, school sectors and geographies. It is not uncommon for students to speak about 'watching something' at school as a point of entry to becoming climate-concerned; documentaries still seem to be a pedagogical point of entry for conversations about climate change in school classrooms.

Yet, how young people feel when they watch documentaries about climate change in their classrooms varies and is affectively ambivalent. Natasha Abhayawickrama, a member of the *Striking Voices* project team, narrates:

> For me, climate change was something I learnt about at a really young age – I have memories from primary school of watching really alarmist videos/ documentaries and essentially interpreting that as 'this is the end of the world'. I was confronted with really existentialist thoughts from a really young age and had severe amounts of climate anxiety.

Watching documentaries alone may just create and exacerbate climate anxiety: distress connected to climate change. Emma Heyink, another young person involved in the project told Natasha and I, during a research conversation, how she first learned of and felt about climate change; this documentary had a different effect to the anxiety that sparked in Natasha:

> **Emma:** We watched the David Attenborough documentary *Life on our Planet* in English when I was in year eight. [...] [H]e went through what will happen in the next 40 years if we don't stop climate change and limit over 1.5 degrees of warming. And it was not very good, obviously. There was lots of floods and fires and everything was going extinct and there were no animals and no food – quite hectic. And [...] after that it was all doom and gloom.
>
> And then there was like a scene after that and it was global climate solutions, like what we can do to stop this. And I was 13 at the time, so I was like, 'Oh my God, this is all so easy. This is all so simple. Why are we not doing this?' And like, obviously there's like politics and stuff behind it, but it all just seemed like this [turn to climate solutions] would make everything so much better for everyone.

For Emma, the documentary spurred her into further considering possible climate solutions, though her later activist experiences tempered her initial enthusiasm that '[t]his is all so simple.' At what point, between the 'climate anxiety' that Natasha recounts, sparked by watching 'really alarmist videos/ documentaries', and the sense that 'this is all so easy' that Emma felt when watching a David Attenborough documentary, did Natasha and Emma feel like they *could* take action on climate? What did these moments in their school classrooms have to do with their later activism outside of school?

Two tendencies in climate change education

Sharon Stein, writing with collaborators from the Gesturing Towards Decolonial Futures (GTDF) arts/ research collective and the Tei das 5 Curas (T5C) network (Stein et al., 2023), synthesises two tendencies in approaches to climate change education. They characterise the first tendency as 'climate doomism': the 'fatalistic sense that it is too late to stop climate catastrophe', associated with 'alienation, apathy, nihilism, and misanthropy' (Stein et al., 2023, p. 988). Natasha's story of her early experiences with learning about climate change exemplifies this tendency and its effects: 'essentially interpreting that as "this is the end of the world"' and feeling 'confronted with really existentialist thoughts'. The second tendency – an attempt to 'counter the rise of climate doomism' – is 'climate solutionism', particularly 'scientific solutionism' (Stein et al., 2023, p. 988). Emma is initially inspired by this 'climate solutionism' approach, when watching a David Attenborough documentary at age 13. Stein and collaborators (2023) acknowledge that 'solutions-oriented climate education may be well intended', but generally reduces climate change 'to a technical problem to be "solved"' while sustaining the underlying *modern/ colonial system*' (988; their italics).

The problem, according to Stein and collaborators, with much contemporary climate education pedagogies, is that they do not foundationally challenge the continuity of this modern/ colonial system. The modern/ colonial 'global system of power' emerged through European colonization and its processes of 'genocide, ecocide, epistemicide, dispossession, subjugation, extraction and exploitation' of peoples and land (Stein et al., 2023, p. 988). To draw attention to this modern/ colonial system is to apprehend the shared roots of the current global system of power and the climate crisis. These colonial processes are also constitutive of the habits of being that contribute to ongoing destruction of peoples and planet: 'prosperity, exceptionalism, innocence, certainty, control, convenience, unrestricted consumption, unaccountable autonomy, epistemic universalism' (Stein et al., 2023, p. 988).

Stein and collaborators express concern that to encourage 'solutions' and actions without individual and collective deep work to dismantle the roots of the current system will perpetuate the logics of this modern/ colonial system. They write that 'many critical pedagogies invite students to be the heroic protagonists of an imagined future' (2023, p. 990) – for example, inviting students to '*take action in the world*', and to understand this heroic action as '*empowering*' (my Unit Plan; *An Inconvenient Truth*). They argue that, if the same habits of being and relating to the world are at work when an 'empowered' young person 'take[s] action in the world', such action risks reproducing 'paternalistic, instrumentalist, and extractive relations between dominant and systematically marginalised communities; ethnocentric imaginaries of sustainability, justice, and change; and simplistic responses that may address the symptoms of complex challenges, but not the root causes' (Stein et al., 2023, p. 991).

Learning climate justice

The more that I have spent time with young people in youth-led climate justice organisational spaces, the more that I have learned about 'climate justice' – as a concept, but also how it looks and feels in teaching and learning spaces beyond school classrooms. 'Climate justice' is not a term that can be found in Australian Curriculum documents. 'Climate justice' binds together climate action with social justice concerns and their shared root causes. The concept of 'climate justice' draws attention to how the communities who are first and worst affected by climate-related impacts are most frequently the communities who have contributed the least to carbon emissions, and how climate change perpetuates and amplifies historical and systemic injustices, particularly for First Nations peoples, people of colour, and low-income communities. To call for climate 'justice' rather than just climate 'action' emphasises the intersectionality of climate change with other forms of injustices, and the need for solidarities across intersecting struggles including racial justice, gender justice, and economic justice. To demand climate justice is to demand that climate solutions and transitions are just and equitable. Climate justice draws attention to the underlying social, economic and political inequalities that exacerbate the impacts of climate change, requiring transformative systems change rather than technocratic and individualising solutions.

Emma describes the power of learning about 'climate justice' in her own personal activist trajectory – learning from older mentor figures in the West Australian Climate Justice Union, and learning about 'The Master's Framework' in a School Strike for Climate training workshop (co-facilitated by Natasha). Natasha has explained, in another book chapter, how the Master's house framework is used in climate justice organising spaces as an educative tool for understanding the climate crisis for her personally:

> [The Master's House] is a visual metaphor of a house (the structure of domination) held up by three foundational pillars: capitalism, white supremacy, and patriarchy. This training included discussion of how corporations and specifically, fossil fuel companies and corporations, are shaped by and benefit from these pillars of oppression. (Abhayawickrama et al., 2024)

Emma explained, in our first research conversation, the pedagogical value of the Master's House:

> It gives you a more justice-centred lens rather than just like: 'climate action.' You've got [to] understand that all those things [different justice issues] link together and you can't look at climate change without looking at all these other issues. It just becomes so much more interlinked and solutions become so much more obvious. [. . .] When people are like, 'oh, climate change is important, but what about all these other issues?' It's like, 'But they're all connected. Like, you can't look at like gender pay gap

without looking at climate change. You can't look about like First Nations justice without [looking at climate change]'.

Emma describes a way of coming to understand contemporary crises historically and in interconnection with each other, in a way that enables her to imagine systemic solutions.

Blanche Verlie (2022, p. 2) writes, in *Learning to Live with Climate Change*, that '[p]ublic and academic approaches to human-climate relations still tend to normalise and advocate scientific modes of climate knowledge, which promote mental comprehension of statistics and graphs through disembodied abstraction'. I think of Al Gore's graphs and wonder if the students in my classroom experienced such 'disembodied abstraction' in relation to the exponential curve. Did my students and I feel temporally and spatially distant from the reality of climate change – climate change as 'out there', somewhere else and sometime later in the future – despite the fact that climate impacts were already being felt in zones of 'high intensity struggle' (Stein et al., 2023, p. 1000, note 4)?

Verlie draws attention to the 'affective climate injustice perpetuated when insulated people turn away from the climate crisis', contrasting:

> … the complacent indifference of such privileged climate deniers and the world-shattering terror and grief of others. [. . .] Those who actively strive to remain unaffected outsource the emotional labour and affective pain of climate change onto others more marginalised, and less complicit, than themselves. (Verlie, 2022, p. 29)

Verlie (amongst other environmental educators) calls for explicit attention to emotions in teaching and learning about climate change – rethinking the relationship between knowledge and feelings and apprehending and centring 'feelings as potent apparatuses for knowing climate' (2022, p. 2). Disembodied cognitive knowledge about climate change – witnessing and chuckling at an ascending exponential graph of carbon emissions – is insufficient; what is needed is another way of thinking, feeling and collectively acting and living in the midst of social-planetary crises (Verlie, 2022). Verlie argues:

> Advocating for affective transformation as a response to complicit people's ecological distress is an effort to cultivate emotional climate justice: to work with emotions for climate justice, and to work towards a more just distribution of the emotional impacts of climate change. (2022, p. 9)

But why isn't it common practice to teach for 'emotional climate justice'?

The risk of courage

It can be challenging, though not impossible, for teachers to bring conversations about climate change into their classrooms, let alone other intersecting social justice concerns. As Susan Groundwater-Smith writes in this volume's opening chapter, 'resistance is risky'. Teachers feel – though unevenly – the weight of escalating performative and accountability demands and time, the disparities of funding and resourcing between school contexts, and the fear of being accused of political indoctrination and/ or emotional manipulation. Social psychologist Carly Trott synthesises the literature around teachers and teaching climate justice: teachers can face 'structural and institutional barriers' to examining climate change in a way that draws connections to issues of social justice and collective action. These barriers include 'limited professional autonomy, lack of resources and support, limited training in teacher training programs and hostile school cultures', though 'the nature and magnitude of systematic and ideological barriers vary widely across contexts' (2024, p. 3). In some contexts, teachers who wish to nurture critical thought, feeling and action in relation to matters of climate change may be fearful of complaints that they are propagating the 'woke agenda'. Such riskiness is not confined to climate change – it is also felt by teachers in relation to teaching other issues to other politicised social justice concerns: sex and gender education, critical race theory, the history and ongoing forces of coloniality, including Palestine, Indigenous knowledge systems and decolonisation.

It is also emotionally risky for teachers to teach climate change. Teachers may be cautious about sparking and fuelling climate anxiety – like Natasha described – and then default to downplaying or skirting around the scale of the crisis, focussing on individual actions that can be taken, or amplifying the 'hopeful' solutions – like Emma described. Stein and colleagues describe three 'modern/ colonial assumptions' that inform these predominant approaches:

1. 'talking about the magnitude of the challenges we face will make people despair or 'give up' (hence education should promise hope)';
2. 'talking about volatility, uncertainty, complexity, and ambiguity (VUCA) will make people feel overwhelmed (hence education should promise certainty and solutions)';
3. 'talking about complicity will make people feel immobilized (hence education should promise innocence)' (Stein et al., 2023, p. 991)

But young people now are exposed to climate change – both in knowledge and through experience – learning from mainstream and social media, and from direct experience of floods, fires and urban heat. Stein et al point out that when young people do 'inevitably confront the depth, complexities, and messiness' of contemporary crises in practice, they may feel 'overwhelmed and immobilized, which is precisely what many educators are trying to avoid by promising projective hope, simplistic solutions, and innocence' (2023, p. 991). Indeed, the school strikes demonstrate that 'many students recognize a growing gap between the world their education was designed to prepare them for, and the world they will inherit, and are, in many cases, 'demanding deeper, more justice-oriented institutional commitments to socio-ecological change' (Stein et al., 2023, p. 988).

But what might it look, sound and feel like to teach climate change differently?

Learning from climate justice pedagogies beyond mainstream schooling

Mainstream schooling might learn from the climate justice pedagogies at work in social movement spaces. In these spaces, climate justice is a living concept, practice and public pedagogy: advocates for climate justice stress the importance of inclusive decision-making processes that involve marginalised communities, particularly those most affected by climate change, and the representation of diverse voices in climate policy discussions and decision-making bodies. Groups who mobilise for climate justice live out horizontal modes of decision-making: these groups emphasise grassroots organising and community-led solutions to climate change, recognising the agency of local communities in designing and implementing initiatives that address both climate change and underlying social injustices. Climate justice campaigns teach multiple publics in powerful critical and affective climate justice pedagogies: critically interrogating politicians' greenwashing statements and their patronising responses to young people's climate concern.

Young people who are involved in these climate justice spaces learn, teach and act in embodied, affective and intellectually rigorous ways. These young people are not just sitting in a classroom, witnessing a 'sage on the stage' explain scientific graphs of escalating emissions. They are collectively teaching and learning from each other and from those directly impacted by climate impacts, sharing and creating stories of social justice and climate change online across viral social media and out-of-school learning spaces. Emma described, in our second research conversation, her recent involvement in intergenerational film nights, 'learning circles', and a book club, to learn and reflect about Palestine and climate justice, in her small coastal town in regional Western Australia:

> It's been really good to be able to create the spaces where people can just learn and reflect, ask questions, and, you know, everything's a lot slowed back down and it's okay if you're confused because you don't have a test on it. It's just like everyone's there to genuinely learn more about an issue and share each other's opinions and things. [...] [F]or school it always feels like it's like it's for a test. [...] Whereas in other solidarity spaces, it feels so much more intent[ional] because you've chosen to go there and you understand that what you're learning and [you know that] grasping those concepts is really important so that you can, incorporate it into life and unlearn some things, learn some new things. [...] Just like unlearning all the white supremacist, imperialist, capitalist principles that have been in a lot of our lives since the beginning because of the way that our education system works or just general society.

This is learning that is 'slowed back down', where it's okay 'if you're confused', and where 'everyone's there to learn more', 'unlearn' and 'incorporate' this learning 'into life.' These are spaces of collective pedagogical experimentation with other ways of learning, teaching, living and relating.

Pedagogical change from the periphery

Political and pedagogical change is slow and hard and, somehow simultaneously, also happens in the moment when one blinks. Rebecca Solnit, in her book *Hope in the Dark*, writes about how change starts behind the curtains of the 'central stage' of political 'action', with changes travelling 'from the edges to the centre' (2016, p. 29). She writes of the 'onstage' figures – here we might remember Al Gore on a cherry picker in front of a studio audience, and the judges and lawyers who 'only ratify change' (2016, p. 29). Since 'so much attention is focused on that central stage', '[t]he routes to the center are seldom discussed or even explored' (29). But for Solnit, it is the behind-the-scene players – for her, 'popular movements', which:

> ... tug the conscience and change the status quo, and it is in these neglected places that radical power lies. There and in the circuitous routes to the centre, where these new ideas cease to be new as they become the script for the actors onstage, who believe they wrote them. (2016, p. 29)

Social movements as sites of political change; they are also sites of pedagogical change. I consider these social movement spaces to be pedagogical spaces of what Stein and collaborators call 'depth education' (Stein et al., 2023, p. 993). Depth education identifies the 'paradoxes, limits and harms' of the modern/colonial educational system 'without assuming we can simply transcend it', and 'invit[es] engagement and experimentation with other educational possibilities (without assuming we can identify or create fixed, universal, and flawless alternatives' (Stein et al., 2023, p. 993).

In my participation in these social movement spaces, I have been confronted with how:

> ... my past pedagogical practices, and the educational systems, structures and curricula within which I have been a complicit participant, are woefully inadequate in contemporary epistemic-material-affective ecologies that are simultaneously post-truth, posthuman and polarised, and fuelled by the continuities of colonialism and fossil-fuelled industrial capitalism. (Mayes, in Lobo et al., 2021, p. 1506)

In acknowledging the inadequacies and complicity in current pedagogies, systems and curricula, I remain curious about the 'radical power' of *school classrooms* for 'tug[ging] the conscience and chang[ing] the status quo' (Solnit, 2016, p. 29). There is radical power in school classrooms that operates multidirectionally: students who challenge and change the politics and practices of their teachers; teachers whose pedagogical practices prick the moral compasses of their students; students who sharpen their parents' and communities' alertness to the urgent need to act. This radical potential of classroom life means that pedagogical courage matters.

Acknowledgements

This essay was written on unceded Wadawurrung Country. This research has been funded through an Australian Research Council (ARC) Discovery Early Career Researcher Award (DECRA; project number DE220100103; 2022–2025), and a Deakin University Alfred Deakin Postdoctoral Research Fellowship (Deakin University, Deputy Vice Chancellor Research; 2020–2022). The project team for the DECRA project includes Natasha Abhayawickrama, Sophie Chiew, Netta Maiava and Dani Villafaña, who are young climate justice activists and employed as Research Associates at Deakin University. Emma Heyink was part of two longer research conversations with Natasha Abhayawickrama and me as part of this project. Deep gratitude and thanks to Natasha and Emma for their insights and all who have participated in this project. The opening section of this chapter expands on a previously published piece (Mayes, in Lobo et al., 2021, pp. 1500–1501).

References

Abhayawickrama, Natasha, Mayes, Eve, & Villafana, Dani (2024). White audacity and student climate justice activism. In: M. Lobo, E. Mayes, & L. Bedford (Ed.), *Planetary justice: Stories and studies of action, resistance, and solidarity*. Bristol: Bristol University Press, pp. 213–231, TBA.

Guggenheim, Davis (2006). *An inconvenient truth*. USA: Paramount Classics.

Lobo, Michele, Bedford, Laura, Bellingham, Robin Ann, Davies, Kim, Halafoff, Anna, Mayes, Eve, Sutton, Bronwyn, Walsh, Aileen Marwung, Stein, Sharon, & Lucas, Chloe (2021). 'Earth unbound: Climate change, activism and justice'. *Educational Philosophy and Theory*, 53(14), 1491–1508.

Solnit, Rebecca (2016). *Hope in the dark: Untold histories, wild possibilities*. Chicago, IL: Haymarket Books.

Stein, Sharon, Andreotti, Vanessa, Ahenakew, Cash, Suša, Rene, Valley, Will, Huni Kui, Ninawa, Tremembé, Mateus, Taylor, Lisa, Siwek, Dino, Cardoso, Camilla, Duque, Carolina 'Azul', Oliveira da Silva Huni Kui, Shyrlene, Calhoun, Bill, van Sluys, Shawn, Amsler, Sarah, D'Emilia, Dani, Pigeau, Dani, Andreotti, Bruno, Bowness, Evan, & McIntyre, Angela (2023). 'Beyond colonial futurities in climate education'. *Teaching in Higher Education*, 28(5), 987–1004.

Trott, Carlie D. (2024). 'Envisioning action-oriented and justice-driven climate change education: Insights from youth climate justice activists'. *Children & Society*, n/a(n/a).

Verlie, Blanche (2022). *Learning to live with climate change: From anxiety to transformation*. Oxon & New York: Routledge.

ACTIVISTS IN RETHINKING HOPE, COURAGE, AND WISDOM

Barry Down

Introduction

When Susan invited me to contribute to this collection of essays, I was in the process of navigating my transition to 'retirement' after 30 years working as a teacher educator-researcher grappling with the changing nature of teachers' work, student dis/re/engagement, educational inequality, and social justice. The opportunity to reflect on my own intellectual journey was both timely and challenging as I tried to make sense of what it means to be an activist educator in the context of the ideas animating this book – hope, courage, and wisdom.

I want to begin by referring to Postman and Weingartner's classic book *Teaching as a subversive activity* (Postman and Weingartner, 1971). My motivation is threefold, firstly, it was one of the few books that excited me as a student teacher back in the 1970s, secondly, it offered a critique of the problems and impediments facing education, and thirdly, it proposed an alternative vision for teaching. The book resonated with me for many reasons – the playfulness of language, the provocations, the metaphors, the social imaginary, the spirit of rebellion and the courage to question the way things are. In essence, Postman and Weingartner were railing against the 'essential mindlessness' of the 'burgeoning bureaucracy' captured in the motto 'Carry on regardless' (p. 24). They argued that bureaucracies, like schools, 'rarely ask themselves "Why?" but only "How?" questions' (p. 24).

Postman and Weingartner were struggling with the fundamental question of what it means to teach? For them, it was about cultivating 'courageous and imaginative thinkers' (p. 13) with 'a high degree of freedom from the intellectual and social constraints of one's tribe' (p. 17). In other words, schools and teachers have a moral responsibility to foster in young people that most subversive of intellectual dispositions – 'the anthropological perspective . . . that allows one to be part of his [sic] culture and, at the same time, to be out of it' (p. 17). This involves developing in young people 'the attitudes and skills of social, political and cultural criticism' (p. 24). Postman and Weingartner invoked Ernest Hemingway's encounter with a reporter about the qualities of a 'good writer' and his reply – 'have a built-in shockproof crap detector' (p. 16), to encapsulate the spirit of the 'good teacher'.

As I thumbed through the well-worn pages of this book, first published in 1969, some key words appeared throughout – curiosity, inquiry, democracy, community, questions, meaning making, relevance, usefulness, problem solving, reality, language, stories, and social worth. These ideas played a significant part in the development of my own sense of criticality about the nature of teaching. In the remainder of this chapter, I endeavour to pursue the legacy of Postman and Weingartner by drawing on the tradition of critical reflection to unpack aspects of my own experience that might be useful in conceptualising the idea of the activist (subversive) educator. Drawing on these experiences I seek to better understand the changes that lay behind my own thinking and practices intellectually and practically.

For me, 'being critical' seeks to address two key questions:

(i) What needs to be struggled against (critique)? and
(ii) What is the alternative (possibilities)?

What needs to be struggled against?

Looking back on my own professional biography I want to share some key observations, questions, struggles and frustrations about what's happening to teaching. These provocations are not designed to be yet another text of despair, but rather 'with a sense of problem, of something going on, some disquiet and of something that could be explicated' (Smith, 2004, p. 9). I take

Freire's (2004) advice that in 'speaking about reality as it is and *denouncing* it, also *announces* a better world' (p. 105).

Dehumanising views of teaching

Like many of my colleagues in the mid-1970s, I commenced my teaching career with a great deal of optimism and hope about making a difference to individual lives and society. The initial excitement of working on school-based curriculum development and community-based activities soon waned, however, as the grammar of schooling overwhelmed any potential for innovation and creativity in the school curriculum. Sadly, these pressures have escalated in recent times under the umbrella of neoliberalism and its corollary corporate managerialism where the emphasis on competition, individualism, accountability, standardisation, testing, benchmarking, and performativity lead to an emaciated and dehumanising view of teaching.

In this context, schools have become increasingly alien and inhospitable places for many students and teachers who are physically and metaphorically leaving the building. I have spent countless hours talking with teachers and students who have become disenchanted, alienated, and cynical about their work. By whatever metric, teachers are struggling with stress, burnout, workloads, attrition, accountability, behaviour, and casualisation. Students too are switching off or dropping out with escalating numbers of suspensions and exclusions, home schooling, school refusal, and mental health and well-being problems.

Decontextualised understandings of teaching

In 1982, I moved to Zimbabwe where I taught history at Highfields Secondary School in a black township on the outskirts of Harare. Arriving shortly after the War of Independence, times were volatile and always interesting. During this time, I learnt two significant lessons about teaching, firstly, education is always political and secondly, context is everything! My crude attempt to teach British colonial history to satisfy the requirements of the British A and O level curriculum and examination system was difficult for myself and my older students, many of whom were part of the struggle. It also collided with the new government's attempt to re-write Zimbabwe's history. These early experiences taught me that history can only ever be a partial account of reality because it depends on who is telling the story. Whose knowledge? Whose interests? Who benefits?

Moving forward a few decades I had the opportunity to be involved in a series of school-based ethnographies. In this work I came up close to the realities of daily life for students and teachers as they struggled with the effects of poverty, unemployment, housing, drug and alcohol abuse, welfare dependency and mental health and well-being. These school communities are euphemistically described as 'disadvantaged', 'low socio-economic status' or 'hard to staff' schools. In these school communities, the free market notion of school choice is in fact a sham because parents do not have the means to enrol their children in well-resourced public or private schools in middle-class suburbs. Australia indeed has one of the most stratified and unequal education systems in the world with profound effects on the least advantaged.

These experiences challenged me professionally and intellectually as I struggled with some major contradictions and tensions about the nature of teaching. I started to understand that teachers are not simply curriculum deliverers, but rather are cultural workers committed to addressing the historical and contextual issues facing their students, schools, and communities. If teachers do not have an awareness of the ideological, philosophical, historical, economic, and political contexts in which they teach, they simply exacerbate feelings of frustration, alienation, disaffection, anger, anxiety, and injustice. Once teachers begin to understand the culture of the community beyond the school gate, then they will be better placed to generate a more relevant, meaningful, and consequential education.

Politicisation of teaching

One of my colleagues relates the story about a politician expressing concern with literacy teaching and why students are performing badly on standardised test scores. It's a topic that consumes considerable column space in local and national newspapers. This senior minister was perplexed with the poor results of NAPLAN and proceeded to compare teaching to servicing a car. If you simply follow the checklist of things to do, like a good mechanic, then everything will be fine. In other words, teaching is perceived to be a technical-instrumental activity which requires teachers to follow a set of prescribed rules and procedures. Viewed in this way, if schools are 'failing' the blame can be sheeted home to poor teachers and teaching methods. Therefore, it is hardly surprising that there have been a reported 101 inquiries into teacher education since 1979 leading to a plethora of recommendations to 'fix' teacher quality.

In this environment, there is a cascading effect as teachers and students are held responsible for their own performance irrespective of the broader social inequalities and circumstances in which they find themselves. When 'good teaching' is calibrated based on standardised test results (e.g., PISA and NAPLAN) it not only fails to acknowledge the complexities of teachers' work but diminishes the craft of teaching to a simplistic checklist of what content, strategies and evaluation techniques teachers should master. This obsession with performativity, comparison, competition, standards, benchmarking, and league tables erodes the relational foundations of education which is supplanted by an instrumental means-end practicality or 'what works'. This approach relies on so-called 'evidenced-based' or 'scientific' research exemplified by John Hattie's *Visible learning: Maximizing impact on learning* as the only form of knowledge that counts.

Instrumentalisation of teaching

While there is an enduring belief that the work of teaching is apolitical, those who attempt to control the nature of education such as international agencies (e.g., International Monetary Fund, World Trade Organisation, Organisation for Economic Co-operation and Development), politicians, governments, education systems, think tanks, and interest groups are less restrained about promulgating all kinds of policies and points of view about teaching. At the top of the wish list is an unshakeable commitment to free market ideologies, competition, and discipline. In this world, education is commodified like any other product and treated within an industrial model of inputs (financial resources) and outputs (improved test results).

The National Professional Standards for Teachers (NPST), for example, construes teaching as a mere practical matter concerned only with content, planning, assessment, management, and reporting. This leads to the portrayal of teachers as technicians responsible for the delivery of predetermined outcomes to be reinforced by a set of accountability and measurement indicators. The problem with management pedagogies is that they assume teachers are the problem and the solution lies in more control and predictability over the 'correct' method while ignoring complexity and context and removing teacher judgement. The only thing left to consider then, is what students are taught (e.g., western heritage, phonics), how students are taught (e.g., back-to-basics), by whom (e.g., 'quality' teachers), and what kind of learning environment (e.g., discipline and control).

What is the alternative – Critical hope?

Against this backdrop, I draw on the idea of 'critical hope' to help reconstruct a more humanising and democratic version of education than exists in the neoliberal policy landscape outlined in the previous section. There are many possible places to start this process of policy reclamation but none better than the writing of Paulo Freire. As Freire (2004) argues, our 'presence in the world' is not simply to "adapt to it", but rather to "transform it" by speaking about our dreams and engaging in practices consistent with it' (p. 7).

Freire believes that hope requires two things – *anger* (rage and indignation) with the way things are and the *courage* to see that they do not remain that way. Central to Freire's (2000/1970) notion of 'hope' is the view that men and women are continually in the 'process of becoming – as unfinished, uncompleted beings in and with a likewise unfinished reality' (p. 84). Viewed in this way, education is an ongoing activity in which people 'come to see the world not as a static reality, but a reality in process, in transformation' (p. 83).

On the other hand, 'hopelessness' (fatalism and determinism) is 'a form of silence, of denying the world and fleeing from it' (Freire, 2000/1970, p. 91). To put this bluntly, Freire argues that 'hope ... does not consist in crossing one's arms and waiting' (p. 92). For him, this kind of passivism is 'empty and sterile' and likely to result in responses that are 'bureaucratic and tedious' (p. 92). To be fully human, therefore, requires a different kind of education, one in which schools become places of 'critical hope', imbued with a spirit of curiosity, humanity, courage, joy, love, compassion, reflection and social justice.

In a similar vein, Greene (2005) argues that what is needed is a shift in perspective, or an alternative way of 'seeing' the world 'big' rather than 'small'. For her, this means 'one must resist viewing other human beings as mere objects or chess pieces and view them in their integrity and particularity instead' (p. 11). Greene's approach is useful because it makes 'transformations, openings, [and] possibilities' more 'audible' (p. 17) as we search for 'new beginnings' (p. 80). She helps us move beyond the diminished focus on 'small' policy thinking which 'screen ... out the faces and the gestures of individuals, of actual living persons' and focus instead on the messy, contextual, pedagogical, relational, and emotional dimensions of teaching (p. 11).

In the context of this radical vision for education, and the cursory detour into some literature, I now turn to consider what kinds of pedagogical, cultural and community conditions need to be created to support the work of activist educators. Drawing on my own experience I will organise this discussion around a series of ideas and practices that have informed my own work over three decades. This is by no means a complete list but a modest attempt to identify and describe what might be helpful in creating an activist teaching profession.

Asking questions

I begin with the fundamental proposition that 'asking questions is a constructive act because it makes change possible' (Shannon, 1992, p. 3). By way of example, I recall two classroom teachers (pseudonyms used) who were troubled by their school's policies around literacy practices and behaviour management respectively. Jane was uneasy about withdrawing students from the classroom for remedial reading lessons. Jane asked her principal why the school organised reading lessons in this way. She was surprised by the response. The principal replied, 'I don't know, but you can change it if you like'. This caused some disquiet as Jane wanted to pursue a research degree investigating the effects of grouping and the removal of students from the classroom. I assured her that the exchange with the principal was not wasted because it revealed something about common sense practices that often go unquestioned.

Mary on the other hand, was troubled by the punitive discipline regime of her school. She spoke out about the school's discipline policies in the hope that it might generate some collegial dialogue. School management, however, interpreted her actions as disruptive and unprofessional. In response, Mary enrolled in a PhD to investigate her experience of behaviour management policies in schools. This led to an insightful school-based ethnography of behaviour management policies from the point of view of students.

I mention these two examples to highlight the importance of questioning taken-for-granted assumptions about teaching and learning. If we wish to create a more engaged and activist learning community in schools, then we must be prepared to create the intellectual and pedagogical conditions for teachers to pursue questions of immediate relevance and worth to their classrooms. This involves pursuing a 'pedagogy of the question' by distancing ourselves from bureaucratic daily existence (Bruss & Macedo, 1985, p. 8) to raise awareness through reflection of 'what is' and by exploring 'what might be' (Simon, 1992, pp. 3–4).

Thinking critically and theoretically

While thinking critically and theoretically can be personally and profession-ally unsettling it lies at the heart of being an activist educator. Of course, there are many obstacles and barriers to critical thought – culturally, intellec-tually, and professionally – because teaching is supposedly apolitical and de-politicised. Despite these conserving tendencies, activist educators are willing to 'speak back' to the prevailing orthodoxies being circulated and enforced by the acolytes of neoliberal policies for education.

When I moved to a small regional university campus in 1987, I was driven by a desire to ask more probing kinds of questions about the moral, ethical, and political purposes of education. Unlike schools, university teaching had many advantages in terms of greater time and freedom to systematically investigate one's interests, to read and think. Nonetheless, there were chal-lenges, including heavy workloads organised around administration, teaching, community service and research. These issues have persisted and intensified over the decades as government funding cuts, staff redundancies, casualisa-tion, corporate governance and metrification have gradually eroded scholarly endeavours.

Nonetheless, finding the space to pursue a PhD gave me an opportunity to better understand the nature of teaching through the sociological lens of the state, class, race, and gender. This spirit of criticality provided an anchor point for the ways in which my teaching and research interests evolved over the next 30 years. This kind of criticality occurs when teachers come together to engage with practice and theory (praxis), not grand theory nor abstracted theory, but theory capable of interrupting the contemporary realities of every-day practices in classrooms.

Creating critical learning communities

During this time, the idea of a 'critical learning community' provided a con-ceptual framework to help me work through my own understandings and frustrations about what was happening to teachers' work. Each of the terms contained in this concept has a particular meaning:

(i) *'critical'* – refers to the process of raising awareness that is predisposed towards social change and social justice based on self-reflection. It also refers to the process of challenging taken-for-granted assumptions about teaching and learning;

(ii) *'learning'* – through self-reflection, collaboration, and dialogue; and

(iii) *'community'* – where connections, relationships and interdependencies are valued.

Henry Giroux's (1988) notion of 'teachers as intellectuals' is perhaps one of the most clearly articulated portrayals of this revitalised conception of teaching. He cultivates the view that teachers are more than low level technicians or clerks implementing the orders of others. Giroux believes that teachers need to create the conditions necessary for them to 'write, research, and work with each other in producing curricula and sharing power' (p. xxxiv). In essence, this means teachers taking control of their work to produce their own knowledge –theories and practices – by shifting the emphasis from questions of what (technical) and how (practical) to also consider questions of why (emancipatory). This kind of critical intellectual activity requires a different sense of purpose to transform the structural, cultural, and pedagogical conditions under which teachers currently work.

In this spirit, I have collaborated with some remarkable teachers and academics wanting to explore the scholarly and intellectual aspects of teachers' work. In this community of learners, dialogical forms of exchange and mutual regard around issues of common concern are fostered while improvisational and experimentational views of teaching and learning are encouraged. By way of example, I was fortunate to work with many like-minded educators under the umbrella of the Commonwealth National Professional Development Project, specifically the Innovative Links Between Universities and Schools for Professional Development (1994–1996). This project provided a set of participatory principles and processes for university and school-based colleagues to collaborate on issues of mutual interest using action research and teacher inquiry approaches. As a young academic my involvement in this project taught me the value of creating spaces and places for teachers to pursue local investigations of relevance to their circumstances and needs.

Drawing on these formative experiences, I invited long-time friends and collaborators John Smyth and Rob Hattam to work with a group of nine teachers studying for their research-based Master of Teaching. Over a period of three years this group of courageous teachers and school leaders would meet two to three times a year to share journal writing, readings, tasks, reflections, and lines of inquiry. John and Rob's critically engaged approach to working with teachers and novice academics provided a refreshing window into how the concept of a 'critical learning community' actual works. Importantly, it provided a more hopeful vision of teaching beyond the narrow constraints of competency-based approaches to teacher's work that were doing the rounds at the time.

Listening to students and teachers

Building on these early experiences I worked on a series of collaborative school-based ethnographies with colleagues to investigate a range of issues including educational participation and retention, teacher resilience, school-to-work transitions, and the role of the performing arts. As the City of Rockingham Chair of Education (2005–2013) I was able to spend considerable time in local high schools listening to young people and teachers describe their experience of school life. These exchanges were grounded in the values of 'voiced research' which provided a space for participants to 'speak back' to decades of neoliberal school reform including school choice, league tables, back-to-basics, residualisation, vocationalisation, and standardised testing.

Each research project started with a commitment and passion to challenge taken-for-granted constructions of the way things are, how they came to be that way, and what is the alternative. Like Denzin et al. (2006) we were committed to building 'a collaborative, reciprocal, trusting, mutually accountable relationship with those studied' so that we might 'positively contribute to a politics of resistance, hope and freedom' (p. 776).

This kind of activist scholarship endeavours to give voice to those most directly impacted by school reform. It provides participants with an opportunity to talk about the things that really matter to them. Drawing on these experiences we endeavoured to describe the conditions that either enable or constrain learning and future aspirations. In this process, we generated portraits of individual lives linked to bigger social issues in ways that allowed us to reframe dominant deficit discourses around perplexing social and educational policy issues, for example, disaffection, disengagement, alienation, mental health, and 'not learning'.

Connecting to students' lives and culture

Drawing on these student portraits we (John Smyth, Lawrence Angus, Barry Down and Peter McInerney) created a rich archive of material to identify the conditions that need to be brought into existence to support an activist and socially critical approach to school and community renewal. We argued that this involves a more expansive understanding of three sets of interrelated themes – culture and community (drawing on local strengths, leadership and resources), structure and organisation (fostering flexible student focussed and supportive school culture by creating spaces for dialogue, reflection and innovation), and pedagogy and curriculum (connecting to students' lives and culture and building relationships based on trust, respect and care).

The schema outlined here is not intended to be yet another check list or set of 'quick fix' interventions but rather a heuristic device to guide local investigations with a view to generating alternative policies and practices. Sitting beneath these ideas though are some disconcerting stories of frustration, disillusionment, alienation, and disaffection. Equally, there are stories of great courage, hope, and optimism among some of the most marginalised young people in society as they attempt to navigate their way in an increasingly fragile, hostile, and precarious world. What shines through in this kind of activist research is the sense of generosity and agency displayed by so many of our research participants, teachers, and community activists all working to create a more socially just school.

Concluding remarks

I want to conclude this essay by invoking Schwartz and Sharpe's (2010) idea of 'practical wisdom' and why it might be useful. As activist educators, we are constantly searching for new insights to address 'popular problems' (thanks to Leonard Cohen). I was struck by the relevance of this idea in the context of teaching which is ultimately a relational activity. Drawing on Aristotle, Schwartz and Sharpe argue that 'neither rules (no matter how detailed and well monitored) nor incentives (no matter how clever) will be sufficient to solve the problems we face' (p. 5). In essence, practical wisdom involves 'performing a particular social practice well ... and that meant figuring out the right way to do the right thing in a particular circumstance, with a particular person, at a particular time' (pp. 5–6). It takes practical wisdom 'to translate the very general aims of a practice [like teaching] into concrete action' (p. 7).

In this sense, teaching is always a hopeful act as it endeavours to navigate the complex entanglements and exchanges between teachers and students who bring their own culture, language, experience, and histories to the classroom.

References

Bruss, N., & Macedo, D. (1985). Toward a pedagogy of the question: Conversations with Paulo Freire. *Journal of Education, 167*(2), 7–21.

Denzin, N., Lincoln, Y., & Giardina, M. (2006). Disciplining qualitative research. *International Journal of Qualitative Studies in Education, 19*(6), 769–782.

Freire, P. (2000/1970). *Pedagogy of the oppressed* (30th Anniversary Edition). Continuum.

Freire, P. (2004). *Pedagogy of indignation*. Paradigm Publishers.

Giroux, H. (1988). *Teachers as intellectuals: Toward a critical pedagogy of learning*. Bergin & Harvey.

Greene, M. (2005). Teaching in a moment of crisis: The spaces of imagination. *The New Educator, 1*(2), 77–80.

Postman, N., & Weingartner, C. (1971). *Teaching as a subversive activity*. Penguin.

Schwartz & Sharpe (2010). *Practical wisdom: The right way to do the right thing*. Riverhead Books.

Shannon, P. (1992). *Becoming political: Readings and writings in the politics of literacy education*. Heinemann.

Simon, R. (1992). *Teaching against the grain: Texts for a pedagogy of possibility*. Bergin & Garvey.

Smith, D. (2004). *Writing the social: Critique, theory and investigations*. University of Toronto Press.

EDUCATION AND DEMOCRACY: TOWARDS A CURRICULUM FOR DEMOCRATIC HOPE

Alan Reid

Introduction

Democracy is in trouble around the world. Indeed, there is a small cottage industry of recently published books with titles which variously describe democracy as being in chains, reaching its twilight, or dying. The common theme is that democratic government is worth saving because, despite its imperfections, it offers the best chance we have for addressing the complex issues facing the world today. This essay accepts that foundation assumption and focusses on the role that education can play in the renewal of democracy in the 21st century.

If, as Aly and Stephens (2022) argue, '(D)emocracy's great virtue is that it offers a perpetually deliberative politics' (p. 56), it isn't a commodity which can be plucked off the shelf at will. Citizens must have the knowledge, skills and dispositions needed to engage with respect, forbearance and reciprocity in democratic deliberation. Without these capacities in its citizenry, democracy is just an empty shell, open to manipulation and distortion by populists and demagogues. Formal education is the major site for the development of democratic capabilities, and yet, if the lack of interest and participation of young people in democratic processes is any guide, formal education is failing in this crucial role.

Disillusionment with democracy is growing and is most obvious among younger generations. A recent study by the Centre for the Future of Democracy at Cambridge University (Foa et al., 2020) – using the largest ever dataset of democratic legitimacy across 160 countries – found that there is a growing gap between youth and older generations on how they perceive the functioning of democracy. By their mid-thirties, over half global millennials say they are dissatisfied with democracy

It appears that this disillusionment is incubating an attraction to authoritarian populism in a number of countries, where populist leaders claim that they represent the interest of the 'real people' and denigrate those who oppose them as being corrupt and illegitimate. Indeed, young people in countries electing populist leaders have increasing levels of satisfaction with this simulacrum of democracy. They view politics as being about 'good' and 'bad' divides, and see people holding opposing political views as morally flawed. More than this, such views become more apparent the greater the level of inequality in a society.

There is no doubt that these trends are making a major contribution to democratic decline. Every year, Freedom House compiles an authoritative report on the state of democracy, using a range of criteria. Its 2023 report described the 17th consecutive year of decline in global freedom where the countries experiencing democratic deterioration outnumbered those showing improvement.

If formal education is central to democracy, what needs to change so that its fundamental contribution to democratic flourishing is realised? Such a question cannot be answered in the abstract, so in this essay I will use Australia as a case study. In particular, I will explore some of the challenges facing democracy in Australia today with a view to suggesting some ways by which formal education can better play its role in democratic renewal.

What is causing distrust of democracy? An Australian case study

According to Freedom House (2023), Australia continues to be one of the countries not yet in democratic decline. Many of the key features central to a democracy – such as free elections supervised by independent electoral commissions, an independent judiciary, a free press, and elected legislatures kept accountable through a range of processes and bodies – are in working order.

And yet a 2019 ANU Election Study (Cameron & McAllister, 2019) found that satisfaction with democracy and trust in government had reached its lowest level on record in Australia since the 1970s. Only one in four Australians said that they had confidence in their political leaders and institutions. And this finding was mirrored by the 2022 Edelman Trust Barometer which found that trust in democracy among Australians had fallen six points since 2021 which was the second biggest decline behind Germany.

How and why is this happening? There are at least three factors that are combining to produce these trends at both State and Federal levels. The first factor relates to the infrastructure of democracy – that is, the institutions and processes which sustain democratic practice in Australia – which are starting to fray at the edges. For example, there are concerns about the lack of diversity of Parliamentary representatives, the fact that party discipline has reduced the possibility for genuine debate, the politicisation of the public service, and the short-term nature of political decision-making which stifles the political will to deal with complex issues and to consider the consequences of legislation for future generations.

The second factor relates to a weakening in political equality, one of the fundamental principles of any democracy. Income and education are major determinants of who can become involved in the political process. Given the growing inequalities in Australian society, many are excluded from participation. For example, if you are not a member of a major party you have to be wealthy to stand for election, or have substantial financial backing; and those with wealth invariably have greater access to power through such mechanisms as paying to attend lunches to meet a minister, giving a large donation to a political party in the expectation of a favourable outcome, or employing lobbyists.

The third factor relates to the debasement of political culture in the public sphere. Representative democracy relies upon an engaged citizenry. This should mean more than limiting democratic involvement to voting every three or four years. Rather, citizens must be willing and able to participate in civil and respectful discussions in public forums informed by a free and open media. Instead, they are largely disengaged from what happens in parliament, and prevented from systematically deliberating about key policy issues.

In addition, where discussion does occur, it is often coarse and contemptuous. Social media has fragmented common sites for public discussion, driving people into silos of sameness where people only talk to those with similar ideas, and misinformation and disinformation is rife. There is often a stronger allegiance to small groups with like interests than to an inclusive and diverse community with a concern to make decisions for the public good. More than this, there is a focus on individual benefits rather than the common good, through artificial intelligence algorithms which hyper-target personal preferences.

These are just a few examples of what is happening, but they are enough to demonstrate why, in Australia, there is a growing distrust of politicians and political institutions, greater division within and between various communities, and a growing sense of alienation and disempowerment among citizens.

The challenge is to restore faith in democracy by addressing the factors which are blighting it, including finding ways to improve the standards of debate and discussion within and between Parliament and the community, increase the levels of trust in our representatives, make our representatives more accountable and political processes more transparent, enhance our electoral systems, and encourage greater citizen participation in democratic processes.

As I argued earlier, education has a key role to play, and yet even a cursory investigation will show that Australian education is falling well short of fulfilling its democratic purpose. As I have explained elsewhere (Reid, 2019) Australian schooling has been ravaged by the ideology of neoliberalism over the past 30 years. At the heart of the neoliberal philosophy is the individual who advances his/her self-interest by competing with others to get ahead. Although Australia followed a softer – 'third way' – version of neoliberal economic policy, beginning in the 1980s, the essence of neoliberalism began to shape our language, the way we see the world and ourselves, and the alternatives that are open to us in the future. By the late 1980s it was permeating all areas of social policy.

In education, neoliberalism appeared in different guises such as policies of school choice and competition, attempts to drive-up results through payment by results, and using standardised tests to compare schools. It has had a number of consequences not the least of which has been the residualisation of public education, segregation of schools by SES and culture, and greater inequality within and between students and their schools.

Elsewhere I have argued that education funding policy must change if the trend to the increasing social segregation of Australian schooling schools is to reverse (Reid, 2019). It has made it much harder for many students to learn to live with and appreciate diversity – a capacity so essential to exercising the reciprocity and tolerance needed to sustain a healthy democracy. In this essay I want to explore the ways in which neoliberal-informed education policy has shaped the school curriculum and damaged the important contribution it can make to democratic flourishing. I will conclude by suggesting some ways to make schooling policy more democratically responsive.

The Australian curriculum and thin democracy

At the level of the formal curriculum, the neoliberal dynamic has had a devastating effect. Not only has it fostered a highly individualistic culture, but so too has it narrowed and standardised the official curriculum. Tests like PISA and NAPLAN have become the main arbiters of educational quality, and educators have been pushed into placing an inordinate emphasis on preparing students for those areas of the curriculum which are tested – and invariably neglecting the rest.

A case in point is the Civics and Citizenship strand within the Learning Area of Humanities and Social Sciences (HASS)which carries almost the sole responsibility of formal education for 'preparing' young people for democratic life. The strand is allocated only about 20 hours per year – or about half an hour of study a week. Not surprisingly the content and skill descriptions are spare, with the major focus being in Years 5–8. Given its brevity, the content amounts to little more than a descriptive outline of Australia's system of government, with barely a nod given to other forms of government, let alone consideration of where Australian democracy is experiencing problems, and where and how citizens might be more deeply engaged in democratic life. In short, Civics and Citizenship education is based on a very thin version of democracy. It assumes that future citizens will be passive voters every three of four years, rather than active participants in public deliberation.

Of course there are schools and teachers who work against the grain of the official strictures and offer a stimulating and engaging civics education program. However this is despite, not because of, the official curriculum, and while ever education for democracy is not valued by policy makers and given the resource support needed, even the best programmes will struggle.

It is little wonder then that the brief encounter with learning about our democratic system that currently exists in the formal curriculum has neither informed nor excited students. The National Assessment Program – Civics and Citizenship conducted by ACER, tests a random sample of Year 6 and Year 10 students every three years about their civics and citizenship understanding. The most recent test reports that only 52.5% of Year 6 students and 42% of Year 10 students are proficient in civics and citizenship knowledge. Whilst associated surveys show that young people care passionately about single issues such as climate change and gender equality, it is clear that they are not equipped to participate fully in Australian democracy by the time they are ready to vote.

In summary if, as I have argued, education is the key to addressing the many problems that are besetting democracy today, the current washed out version of Civics and Citizenship education in the official Australian curriculum is woefully inadequate for that task. A reconfigured approach to education for democracy based on a thick version of democracy is needed.

Hope and courage: Towards a curriculum that supports and sustains thick democracy

A new approach to education for democracy should aim to encourage students to recognise that democracy is the one system of government where citizens are able to engage collectively in making decisions about the condition of their common lives and foster hope for a better future. Rather than limiting the participation of citizens to simply voting every three of four years, this thick version of democracy means that citizens must have the capacities and the will to collaborate with others in a range of forums.

A curriculum for thick democracy needs to be based on, and developed through, a number of principles that will help to ensure that there is not a reversion to the safety of the traditional approach. A central principle is that the curriculum should be developed and implemented democratically. This means going beyond the usual 'expert' panel developing a draft and engaging in desultory consultation before promulgating the final product for implementation every few years. Rather there should be approaches which engage students and teachers in reviewing and co-designing the official framework which guides what happens at the level of the school. Importantly such a framework must itself provide space for co-design to happen at the level of the classroom, allowing the local context to shape programs and activities.

Another important principle is to formally recognise that since an education for democracy is one of the key purposes of education, it should occupy more than just a small place in one Learning Area of the official curriculum. Instead, it should permeate and inform many aspects of all schools and the systems they inhabit. This essay will focus on the intended curriculum, meaning that learning which is consciously designed. I will argue that a new approach could be formulated across four curriculum sites.

Curriculum site 1: The official curriculum – Civics and citizenship Education

The most obvious place to start a new approach to educating for democracy is with the officially designated HASS strand: *Civics and Citizenship Education*. Since States and Territories can adapt the Australian Curriculum to suit local circumstances, it is quite possible for one or more jurisdictions to make significant changes now. If policy makers are serious about the democratic purpose of schooling, the first step must be to increase the time allocation and the scope of Civics and Citizenship Education in the official curriculum across all year levels. That being the case, what is needed to insert a thick version of democracy into the official curriculum?

The curriculum design must be based on an understanding of what democracy entails. This sounds obvious and yet most curriculum documents simply *imply* an understanding, rather than articulate it. As I observed earlier, the current Australian Curriculum is descriptive of the current structures and processes of our representative democracy. Learners are not invited to consider alternative versions of representative democracy, let alone investigate other democratic models such as direct or deliberative democracy.

Any education programme designed to educate for democracy must ensure that the crucial elements of democracy are represented in the official curriculum. These include the foundation values and principles which are common to any democracy and without which democracies exist in name only, such as political equality, freedom of speech, respect for human rights, freedom of association, movement and belief, and tolerance of difference and opposing ideas. It must also include the formal structures and processes that are essential to democracy, and how and where opinions are expressed and political judgments are made by citizens and conveyed to their representative institutions. Importantly, students must learn that these elements are not unchanging givens, but are humanly constructed, evolving over time as contexts change through democratic deliberation.

Another aspect of any new approach involves a focus on pedagogy. Unfortunately the official Australian Curriculum is described separately from suggestions about teaching approaches that might assist its implementation. In a new version of education for democracy, I would encourage teachers to share pedagogical ideas and resources as they experiment with ways to enliven student learning.

One key pedagogical approach is to connect to the life worlds of students through issues that really matter to them. That is, a study of democracy starts to make sense to students when the relevance to their lives can be demonstrated. An education for democracy must involve issues-based investigations leading to action by students. For example, students can work together identifying issues in their local community (or how larger global issues are playing out locally), trying to understand the nature of the issue, the power dynamics involved, and the various possible actions that can be taken.

As they do this, students are learning about the decision-making structures of their democracy. They move backwards and forwards between the issue and the infrastructure available to resolve it, and what avenues exist to express views and take action. At the end of such a study students will reflect not only on the issue, but on institutions and power, and the role of the citizen in a democracy.

Curriculum site 2: School culture

A thick version of democracy rests on democratic hope, meaning that it imagines ongoing interaction between citizens as they define and redefine possible collective futures. In other words, citizens must move beyond a culture of self-interest where public discourse is marred by disdain, resentment and contempt, towards one where citizens lean into one another, exchanging points of view and disagreeing where they must – but doing so respectively, truthfully, and with patience and forbearance. These are fundamental aspects of any healthy democratic culture.

Establishing the conditions for a common life requires an understanding of the kind of culture to which we aspire and a commitment to the ongoing work of developing and employing the dispositions needed to sustain it. This demands skills and dispositions that cannot be acquired in a hit-and-miss way. I want to suggest that the development of the dispositions and practices needed for a healthy democratic culture should be the *daily work* of every year level, in every aspect of every school, as well as education systems. The dispositions should become the cultural air that is breathed.

How might this happen? There needs to be a broad agreement about the dispositions and practices needed to enable the interchange of views and ideas – these include empathy, generosity, frankness, compromise, respect, tolerance, truthfulness, moral hesitation – as well as the skills of attentiveness and a genuine commitment to understanding alternative viewpoints. And then educators must encourage students to develop and use these skills and dispositions in a range of forums where interactions occur – classrooms, the school yard, the community and so on – but also model these in their own structures and interactions. That is, an education system which values its role of educating for democracy will ensure that its decision-making structures are democratic and encourage respectful deliberative exchange in the school.

In other words, the project of creating a democratic culture in a school and education system involves nurturing citizens who have the skills and dispositions to create and sustain the conditions for democratic deliberation. It will require skill and perseverance on the part of all members of the school community, since it is only when it becomes habitual that it can be called a disposition. The importance of this ongoing work cannot be overstated since not only will it change the culture of schools and systems, but ultimately it will address those factors which are so corrosive of the democratic culture in our democracy.

Curriculum site 3: Skills for democratic engagement across the curriculum

There are many skills needed for productive democratic engagement and clearly these cannot all be developed within a single strand of a single Learning Area. A crucial weapon in an education for democracy is an across-the-curriculum approach using some or all of the Learning Areas. There are many ways this can happen, but I will describe two examples.

Earlier I mentioned that one of the challenges facing democratic life is the amount of misinformation and disinformation, fake news, propaganda and conspiracy theories which are permeating public debate. It confronts a fundamental condition of democratic politics – that public discussion in the public sphere is underpinned by FACTS. Of course distortions of factual information were ever present in the political life of industrial society, but the speed and reach of digital technology spawned by the Fourth Industrial Revolution has turned it into being a genuine threat to the very possibility of democracy.

Citizens should have such skills as being able to discern propaganda, identify the authority of any source, weigh up evidence and be sceptical about claims. Every Learning Area is an avenue for developing such capacities. For example: Media Studies is an obvious way to show students how misinformation, disinformation and 'fake news' is represented in mainstream and social media, and how it can be detected; Mathematics can illustrate how statistics can be distorted to create 'facts' used for particular ends; Science can demonstrate how conspiracy theories can be tested using the scientific method; and the study of English and History can be excellent ways to discern how propaganda is developed and used.

The key thing here is for staff at a school to appreciate the threats posed by false information and propaganda, and identify the knowledge, skills and capacities that are needed to resist them. Using that information, staff can collaborate in a whole-school project to identify what each learning area can deliver, and at what year level, and then ensure that there is periodic review of outcomes.

The second example relates to the fact that most of the key issues today cannot be understood from a single disciplinary perspective. They require an ability to understand an issue holistically and a capacity to integrate key concepts drawn from a number of learning areas. If citizens are to actively participate in discussion in the public sphere, they must have some experience in interrelating knowledge across a range of disciplinary boundaries. If an education for democracy is to equip young people with the tools to understand contemporary public issues and play a role in society's response to them, it is important that educators collaborate across the borders of Learning Areas, so that students are able regularly to examine issues from an interdisciplinary or multidisciplinary stance.

Curriculum site 4: Students as engaged citizens now

The dominant discourse in education, and specifically in Civics and Citizenship education, is that the curriculum represents a preparation FOR citizenship. That is, students are citizens in waiting who cannot have a real say in the polity until they turn 18 and can vote. I will argue that whilst an approach to education for democracy must have in mind the knowledge and skills that young people will need when they formally play a part in the polity, it must also recognise that their voices can inform our democracy in some important ways NOW.

Many young people want a say in public forums, but are frustrated because they are either marginalised or dismissed. They can see that decisions being made today are going to have consequences for them, and yet they are being made by people who won't be around when the decisions bear fruit. It is time for the voices of young people to be heard.

Some countries like Wales have passed legislation which requires their Parliaments to consider the impact of every piece of legislation on future generations; and established Commissioners for Future Generations. These are important steps, but they don't fully recognise the role that education can play in engaging students in the public sphere. In some places Youth Parliaments have been established but they tend to involve only a small handful of students, and inevitably they comprise young people who already have a number of advantages.

Is it possible to maximise the voice of young people in the public sphere today, as well as develop their democratic skills for tomorrow? I think that there are any numbers of ways by which this could happen, and once again schools and curriculum are central. However I need to stress that I am not talking about role playing or other simulations. The intention of what follows is to propose mechanisms through which students can project their views in ways that contribute to real decision-making now. For example:

- Why couldn't schools establish multiple sites for student Voice such as class Voices to School Board; or year level Voices to the local Council? In both cases students could trial different models of obtaining representatives (e.g., by election or by lot), different time periods between elections, and different ways to elicit community and class views about identified issues. For example, the Voice to local Council might involve interviewing residents, holding street meetings, and attending Council meetings and presenting. The various Voice forums could be used to organise a Youth Voice to State Parliament;
- Why couldn't local politicians use the model of citizens' juries or citizens' assemblies to engage young people from schools in their electorate in discussing a key piece of legislation before state and federal Parliament, and relay their thoughts to the Parliament?;

- Why not engage students in an annual democracy audit of their school, local area or state and issue a report to the relevant authorities about changes needed?;
- Given the demise of local newspapers, why couldn't students develop a digital version of their own local paper covering local issues, and distribute this via the internet to local residents?

In all these cases, schools would be the base from which this hive of activity is generated, and also the places where considered reflection about what is happening and what students are learning is undertaken. But the point is that such approaches are not simply educational tools – although they are that in spades – but also ways by which young people can have their voices heard today on issues that matter to them. It would inject into our democracy fresh voices and insights which would truly enrich democratic life and foster democratic hope.

Conclusion

I have argued that developing the capabilities needed for an active engagement in democratic life is a role of schooling, par excellence. However, such an aspiration cannot be achieved through serendipity, or by drip feeding some civic facts for a few hours each year, or by a one-off subject in the senior school curriculum. Rather it demands an ongoing immersion in democratic life, where the multi-faceted capabilities needed for active and informed citizenship are developed systematically as a central component of the school curriculum at all year levels. Only a total rethink of traditional approaches to what has been called Civics Education will enable this to happen. It is a crucial task if the current threats to democracy are to be replaced by democratic hope.

References

Aly, W., & Stephens, S. (2022). Uncivil wars: How contempt is corroding democracy. *Quarterly Essay*, 87, 1–71.

Cameron, S., & McAllister, I (2019). *The 2019 Australian federal election: Results from the Australian election study*. Australian National University. https://australianelectionstudy. org/wp-content/uploads/The-2019-Australian-Federal-Election-Results-from-the-Austral ian-Election-Study.pdf

Foa, R. S., Klassen, A., Wenger, D., Rand, A., & Slade, M. (2020). *Youth and satisfaction with democracy: Reversing the democratic disconnect?* Centre for the Future of Democracy.

Freedom House. (2023). *Freedom in the world report, 2023.* https://freedomhouse.org/sites/defa ult/files/2023-03/FIW_World_2023_DigtalPDF.pdf

Reid, A. (2019). *Changing Australian education: How policy is taking us backwards and what can be done about it.* Allen and Unwin.

LEADING A PEDAGOGY OF HOPE
Linda O'Brien

In this essay I give an account of leading colleagues to build shared enthusiasm and optimism about future possibilities for supporting student success. I also conceptualise the work that this takes as a pedagogy of hope. In articulating my vision of a more hopeful school experience for students, I draw on my own practice as a school principal. I believed my job was to articulate a vision of this destination and develop strategies to support the school on this journey. The route may have diverted along the way in responses to resistance or creativity from students, teachers and the community, but hope focussed our collective purpose and inspired innovative solutions, rich curriculum, a sense of belonging and social cohesion. This essay describes that journey and its resistance to narrowly measuring student success, instead learning what students know and how to excite their curiosity about what else they could know.

Leading hope

As educators we support students to engage in learning that provides them with the resources they need to live meaningful lives in the future. At least we might hope that this is what we are doing. But are we always successful? Are some students limited rather than enabled by their schooling? Many school leaders face the challenge of improving engagement in learning. Together, leaders and teachers can make school more relevant and accessible to students. Many students choose to learn alternative skills and knowledge to those offered at school because they do not recognise themselves in the school curriculum, or they feel they have failed to thrive. What do students hope for, what hope do they have of realising their potential futures, and how might we as educators use hope to transform teacher practice and student potential?

As knowledge sources change it has been suggested that schools are becoming increasingly irrelevant as sites for learning and that, as the means for access to learning becomes more flexible, school as an institutional portal through which knowledge can be transported is becoming more dissociated from learning (Goding, 2012; Rincon-Gallardo & Elmore, 2012). For example, knowledge is readily available through different cultural lenses and through digital media, and thus opportunities for learning are more diverse than those offered within schools. Schools can recognise this diverse knowledge by listening to students, and by giving them more agency through structuring the curriculum to make the content more relevant, enjoyable and engaging and thus support individuals and societies to hope for a better future.

What then of a theory of learning in a school context? In this essay I reflect on my own practices as a leader of learning in a high school for boys, and articulate the vision for change that shaped my view of what a school can be and accomplish. I think of these practices as a *pedagogy of hope*; as a commitment to a possible future for the school, the teachers, the curriculum, the community, social relations, and most importantly, for the students.

This story of change is not a story of hope as fantasy or romance, but a story of the strategic practices through which hope for more effective and relevant learning might be realised. These strategic practices involved pragmatic and programmatic interventions into: the forms and functions of schooling; the shape and purpose of different forms of knowledge and ways of knowing; teacher practice and student outcomes. As the new school principal leading a boys' secondary school functioning in challenging socio-economic circumstances in the fourth term of 2008, I began prioritising interventions systematically and strategically to improve the social conditions at the school. Approaching reform from two different but complementary directions, I planned to change the practice of both teachers and students. I aimed to enable teachers and students to participate in learning partnerships and collaborations that challenge inequality and ensure that learning was oriented to social justice. A holistic approach to building this critical awareness aimed to change practice. My approach to change was advanced on multiple fronts, and through a coherent and structured set of practices informed by the work of Pierre Bourdieu's sociology of education.

As a school principal my leadership lessons came not only from Bourdieu, but from the students, the teachers and the community in which I served. I understood that historically and politically, our school, like all other schools, had a particular social function to educate students so that they were equipped for a life within broader social and economic fields. As a starting point I did not critique this function, as I recognised that I had a responsibility to students to support them and bridge the social function of schooling within their own lives in the most meaningful way possible. I had to work within the existing structures and thus consultation, collaboration and negotiation were necessary to frame a collective understanding of the curriculum and how it is taught. If I assumed that students are curious about things, then I believed we had a responsibility to ask them what they were curious about. From their engagement and educational outcomes, it was obvious that they were not always curious about the things the school wanted them to be curious about. It was also clear that their knowledge and interests had often been positioned by teachers as inferior. Additionally, in a stratified school system, their school was considered to be inferior. What hope did these children have?

One way to achieve such hope, is through a negotiated curriculum. However, negotiating the curriculum with students often challenges the practice of teachers and the expectations of the community. Fostering collaboration and communication amongst staff and students helps teachers identify strategies to face these challenges and inspire one another to become effective innovators. In our school, opportunities to develop and change pedagogy to increase student engagement led to the development of an organisational structure we named *The Platform for Collaborative Education* (PCE).

Evolving a platform for collaborative education

The PCE emerged from school-based research to inform its development and implementation and was conducted in two stages; first in 2011 as a situational analysis of the school that would underpin the structuring of the PCE, and then as an evaluation of the effectiveness of the PCE in 2014.

The theoretical foundation of the Platform was based upon the work of Pierre Bourdieu. Bourdieu's (Bourdieu & Passeron, 1977) theoretical concepts of *habitus*, *field* and *capital* helped me to think about the idiosyncrasies of individual schools and the differences in individual teachers' practices and in students' behaviour. *Habitus*, understood as dispositions that reflect the way in which people perceive and respond to their world, is structured by the socialised norms that guide individuals' behaviour over time. These norms are structured by the institutional structures, or *fields*, within which individuals interact. In these *fields*, particular knowledges, or *capital*, are hierarchically valued, and this *capital* determines the ways in which power within *fields* is socially and culturally created. Bourdieu argues that the function of school is to socialise people into certain practices that reproduce certain knowledges that are seen to be of certain value at a particular moment in time. However, for many students, the knowledges and practices that comprise the expectations, or rules of the game, of education are unfamiliar because they have not successfully acquired the necessary *cultural* and *social capital* that is valued and exchanged within the schooling system. Viewed from the perspective of social class and relations of power, 'school' does not work for many students because the knowledge that is mandated is not always accessible or relevant to them (Apple, 2004). However, given that students are required by law to come to school, and so have little choice in being there, the job of school leaders is to help them capitalise on the experience whilst they are there. In the school, as *field*, teachers and students can collaboratively build their knowledge, and students can be given opportunities to share what they know as part of the collaboration. This knowledge becomes a foundation to further investigate, explore and build new *capital*. This potential to explore and build new possibilities is what I refer to as a *pedagogy of hope*.

A pedagogy of hope

This exciting and liberating pedagogy involved regular school-developed and school-based professional learning and provided opportunity for teachers and students to critique the curriculum and examine: what counts as knowledge; how knowledge is communicated; and how knowledge is evaluated. In this way both teachers and students were able to find legitimate reasons for valuing different knowledge and for aspiring to different futures. Through adopting the Platform of Collaborative Education, the 'production of values' about the knowledge, behaviour and aspirations that the school adhered to were to be simultaneously aligned with and counterposed against those constructed within the broader field of education. A constructivist approach aimed to align the values of the students with the values of the teachers and tutors, and to produce social cohesion and improve student engagement more broadly. Engagement or disengagement arose from the social structures in the social and political context, particularly the production of ability that is credentialed with academic achievement. The students who achieved impressive academic results may have done so in classrooms where there was a high level of disruption, or indeed may not have participated in the lessons at all. Questions then arose about which conception of engagement was most meaningful and who benefited, or was excluded, from schooling.

Where high academic achievement is the outcome of a limited syllabus and competitiveness at school, the value of the capital, outside the prevailing norm that many students hold, can be diminished. The power of the pedagogic authority that is asserted by such social structuring can result in students' disengagement with the content of the syllabus, and they turn their attention to devising their own 'fun'. Resistant behaviour to the authority of the school contests the devaluation of their existing *social capital* and they often behave in ways that they believe will win approbation from their peers in order to regain some *capital* of their own. Students use this capital to reproduce practices that are intelligible and acceptable to one another and recognised by others in the group. These capitals may be at odds with the capitals valued by broader systems of education and school leaders and teachers.

The issue of chronically poor academic achievement for the students in the school was reflected in boys' schools with similar demographics. Accordingly, with language teaching in our school, attempts were made to produce (and reproduce for students) the rules for defining the right way to apply a repertoire of devices or techniques to among other matters reading and writing.

Towards more hopeful literacy practices

When we considered prevailing literacy practices the relationship between the structures and these practices concealed the differences in understanding of the socio-cultural histories of the teacher and the student. This different understanding, or misunderstanding, emerged from a situation in which certain language forms were privileged, and where this language alone gave students access to standardised measures of educational success. However, non-prestigious knowledge can also be asserted in the school in order to enable students to experience success at school. I believed that when this different knowledge was mobilised, students are were more likely to participate in the 'business of school', and enthusiastically explore other knowledge, including the knowledge mandated by the curriculum and testing regimes. Critical reflection on teaching practices, and the transaction of privileged knowledge, was a necessary leadership practice for effecting change to students' practice.

The students' relation to both the academic and the everyday language used by the teacher is set against the teachers' understanding of both. Students who are most successful at the reproduction of the language presented to them at school are those who are closest in socio-cultural backgrounds to that of the teacher. At our school, many students did not proficiently access the academic language of the curriculum and instruction. In order to support students to gain greater access to the language presented to them, deliberate measures were taken, including the employment of a culturally diverse staff and an emphasis on literacy education. Literacy education was structured so that teachers scaffolded language understanding and deconstructed textual features so that students were able to recognise and reproduce the forms of language presented to them in class. Explicit instruction supported a dialogue between teachers and students as each received feedback throughout the lessons.

There were, however, barriers to this learning and critical reflection on the practices that generated the structuring of the processes of knowledge. These barriers resulted from a process of social differentiation that perpetuated inequality.

A reflexive stance for the teachers would, I believed, assist them to know the ways in which their pedagogy constructed the students through the intersection of pedagogic authority and the work of the everyday practices of schooling. In order to challenge and change the everyday and taken for granted structures of the school, new practices were implemented. Time for collaboration and communication was considered an essential element of leading change in the school, and this underpinned the structural and strategic model that was adopted.

The courage to change behaviour

It was perceived that new structures and strategies were required to change behaviour and practices. This re-alignment was, in part, informed by a 2009 research project conducted in the school. The purpose of the research undertaken by Groundwater-Smith & Needham as academic partners was to align student and teacher perspectives on what constituted positive and productive behaviours at school. They found that there was a perception amongst some students that through defying instructions they, and not their teachers, controlled the conditions for learning in the school. Students legitimated their defiance and resistant behaviour as a means of developing their sense of identity within their peer culture (Groundwater-Smith & Needham, 2009). Although the school's stated values promoted a belief in 'looking out for each other' and non-violence, the world in which students lived was developed from one another, and inevitably students learnt different values from those encouraged by the school. Some students intimidated others with threats of physical violence and there was a strong belief in some groups that 'you stick together and do not snitch on your mates. If your mate is in trouble, you fight.' (Year 11 student, 2009). 'Your mates' are not only your friends, but they may include boys of the same ethnic background. While some students maintained this sense of power, other students felt unsafe and threatened by these behaviours and did not trust the school to care for their safety.

The combination of antisocial behaviours and disengagement from lessons presented the school with both a pedagogical challenge and a need to address the impact of the chronic underachievement of learning outcomes and antisocial behaviour on individual students. This antisocial behaviour and disengagement gave school leaders and teachers insight into the ways in which they structured student dispositions. To improve student participation in learning, my goal as principal was to influence the social relations between the players in the field in order to produce a positive climate and culture in the school, and a learning environment that was more socially cohesive. I attempted to structure the school so that the worlds of both students and teachers was better understood, and that this understanding had mutual benefits for student and teacher learning. A relational approach was also necessary to gain an understanding of the ways in which the knowledge from the community could be valourised and converted into what may be called the *symbolic capital* within the school.

As a New South Wales (NSW) public school, I understood that the school existed within a broader field of education that not only provided policy direction for the operational structures of the school, but also structured the power and authority of the school to transact the knowledge of the mandated curriculum. Policy is not static; it moves from national and state education department bureaucracies towards the standardisation of education through the national curriculum, national testing for literacy and numeracy and national professional teaching standards. Such policies and practices of standardisation attempt to focus school leadership and management on accountability measures and comparative data. These policies and practices assume a meritocratic hierarchy for teachers, students and schools' performance, as measured by the (Australian) National Assessment Program for Literacy And Numeracy (NAPLAN). In this hierarchy, our school was in the bottom quartile for student performance nationally.

Towards a more collaborative environment employing the voice of students

It has been recognised that young people can make a significant contribution to the development of policies and practices within the schools in which they are the 'consequential stakeholders'. Thomson and Gunter (2006) when working with students as co-researchers in the United Kingdom, and Holdsworth working in schools in Australia (2001), demonstrated the efficacy of students' participation in the evaluation of school systems and learning programs. The power of engaging young people in school-based inquiry cannot be overestimated. Students, having spent a large part of their young lives in classrooms of one sort or another, have a considerable investment in schooling, and deserve to 'have a say' in those educational arrangements. It has been argued that where students have agency, a sense of belonging, and are recognised as competent, they gain a stronger sense of their own abilities and build awareness that they can make changes in their schools, not only for themselves, but also for others. In the past, young people themselves were either not consulted at all, or at best, treated only as a data source. Raymond (2001) has noted that there are a number of steps that can be done when consulting with young people about their education: discussion, where young people are active respondents; dialogue, where they are co-researchers; and, giving their voice significance, where they are researchers, initiating, inquiring, interpreting, and developing actions. It is my contention that to support student negotiated learning, teaching practices need to change from teacher-directed tuition to understanding the teacher as facilitator. This pedagogical shift is a challenge for school leadership teams, teachers, and students and is a necessary one when establishing a pedagogy of hope.

As indicated above, the Platform for Collaborative Education (PCE) was a response to the challenges of leading meaningful change for students, teachers and their community. It was developed from reflection on how to approach change in school operations on a holistic basis, rather than with only those teachers who were willing to develop innovative projects for some students. The PCE was an inclusive whole-school leadership project aimed at the organic development of changes in practices to engage with the challenge of student disengagement from learning.

The PCE did not seek to subvert or reject the educational policy agenda – we had no choice but to follow it. However, it did seek to critique and resist normative assumptions about the socio-cultural knowledge that is transacted in the school, by systematically addressing the issues of curriculum and the social structures that position the school at the bottom of the social hierarchy.

To improve the learning environment, meticulous attention was paid to building relationships between the students and the senior executive (including principal and three deputy principals). This necessitated that the executive be out of their offices and highly visible around the school, engaging with students and getting to know their names. Attention was paid to improvements in the physical amenity of the school, including the refurbishment of classrooms, timetabling, curriculum offerings and relocating faculties. Recognition of positive behaviour of the students was formally instituted in the school led by a team of teachers; the Positive Behaviour Interventions and Supports (PBIS) Team. In-house, scoped and systematic, teacher professional learning was provided to enable teachers time to think about their practices. Both these strategic directions aimed to build teacher capacity through the support of the senior executive of the school. I believed that improving staff morale would enable teachers to build effective relationships with their students as the foundation for effective teaching and learning. All round it required a courageous departure from the taken-for-granted procedures for school management.

As already indicated another vital aspect of school improvement was engaging and representing student voice in school organisation and curricula. Structures needed to be in place to enable this to happen. A systematic overhaul of all aspects of the school ensued, rather than a piecemeal, ad hoc attempt to introduce single programs to ameliorate issues of student engagement. The PCE developed from a systematic and comprehensive overhaul of school leadership and management through research-led practice. A vital component of the new leadership and management structure was the additional school funding from the NSW Low Socio-economic Status (SES) School Communities National Partnership, [a component of The Smarter School Partnership Agreement between the Australian and NSW governments (Department of Education and Communities, 2011)], to provide additional staffing to allow for flexible management of time.

A widening gyre of hope

To keep the focus on improving student learning outcomes, I attempted to balance strategic and operational parameters and adapt to the responses of others within the community. My leadership focus was on developing and sustaining effective relationships with all members of a dynamic school community in a poor neighbourhood and building a commitment to collaborative problem solving for successful learning. After the inception of the PCE, the curriculum flourished. Teachers innovated and worked in partnership with students to co-construct learning. Partnerships with cultural institutions, community organisations, universities and business provided learning opportunities to evaluate the curation of exhibits at museums, libraries, and art galleries; participate in creative writing workshops and have works published; compose and perform their own music at major events and performance venues; partner with business to create the Pulse Café; pursue the art of barbering in partnership with a major arts organisation and create a barber shop. University partnerships enabled students to become pseudo clients for architecture students at the University of Sydney and advise on relandscaping the school. Work at Macquarie University led to the development of a robotics program which enabled students to compete internationally in interschool robotics competitions. Partnerships with community organisations, particularly Sydney Youth Connect, supported social cohesion and improved students' sense of belonging as well as providing a cultural link between families and the school. Performing arts, particularly music, was a major focus area and student performances were a source of pride at school celebrations and community events. Food preparation engaged students, parents and staff in close collaboration when celebrating religious and other community events.

To evaluate the changes that were made in the school I conducted regular conversations with all teachers and consulted with student groups. Teachers spoke with passion about their moral purpose and their strong desire to make a difference to the students in their classes. The transformative goal of their job for many of them had an ethical framework that arose in part from working in a school that serves a low socio-economic community. At the same time their passion for their subject discipline, be it English or Mathematics or Science, was evident in these discussions. The knowledge that they were transacting was core to their job. Through their education they had invested in knowing their discipline and acquiring practical efficiency as teachers. This practical efficiency structured their *habitus*, which developed as they gained recognition and distinction for their practice. This recognition came from the student achievement of the learning outcomes set out in the programs and from acknowledgement of their work by those who had higher positional authority, such as the principal.

This wonderful school culture of creativity, excitement, diversity and commitment was fuelled by hope from all members of the community. The school continues to provide opportunity for students to succeed in an innovative curriculum that changes and adapts as members of the whole school community consult and collaborate to find solutions. Such collective engagement and change are the very foundation for hope.

References

Apple, M. (2004). *Ideology and curriculum*. Routledge.

Bourdieu, P (1977). *Outline of a theory of practice*. Cambridge University Press.

Bourdieu, P. & Passeron, J. (1977). *Reproduction in Education, Society and Culture*. London: Sage.

Goding, S. (Producer). (2012). Richard Elmore on education reform. *Education Policy – Aspen Institute Washington, DC*.

Groundwater-Smith, S. & Needham, K. (2009) *Student and Teacher perspectives on positive behaviour management*. An unpublished research report.

Holdsworth, R. et al., & Melbourne Univ. Youth Research. (2001). Student Action Teams: An Evaluation 1999–2000. Working Paper 21.

Raymond, L. (2001). Student involvement in school improvement; from data source to significant voice. *Forum, 43*(2), 58–74.

Rincon-Gallardo, S., & Elmore, R. (2012). Transforming teaching and learning through social movement in Mexican middle public schools. *Harvard Education Review, 82*(4), 471–490.

Thomson, P., & Gunter, H. (2006). From 'consulting pupils' to 'pupils as researchers': A situated case narrative. *British Educational Research Journal, 32*(6), 839–856.

THE TRANSFORMATIVE POWER OF TRUTH-TELLING: FOSTERING HOPE, COURAGE, AND WISDOM IN STUDENTS

Dr Cathie Burgess and Kylie Captain

Truth telling is critical if we are to understand, acknowledge and respect Aboriginal and Torres Strait Islanders' (henceforth referred to as Aboriginal people, as this is written on Aboriginal land and respectfully includes Torres Strait Islander peoples as per educational policy in our jurisdiction) lived experiences of colonisation, and how they are represented in Australian society today. Finding optimism and hope for young people in schools must come from a place of truth and the courage to listen deeply to our nation's true history and join in a journey of healing with Aboriginal peoples.

Truth telling is tough, uncomfortable, unsettling and distressing – hard to tell and hear. For young non-Aboriginal preservice teachers about to embark on a teaching career in the face of relentless criticism of teachers and schools, it is a watershed moment where emotional investment is more important than anything they have learnt about their discipline and how to teach it (Thorpe et al., 2021). Many wonder why they chose teaching until they listen to Aboriginal Elders recounting their lived experiences of tragedy and trauma, and through the generosity of the truth tellers, find hope and courage to make a difference when they begin their careers. This is clearly articulated by a preservice teacher who participated in LFC experiences at university.

I had spent my life going with the mainstream flow that turned a deaf ear to these stories because they were not given any airtime by commercial media or were too difficult to listen to. While my parents are a product of their own upbringing, my silent pledge to the Uncles is that my own (still young) children, and any young people that I teach, will hear the truth from me on these events.

The impact of colonial education on schooling

The 'Great Australian Silence', a term coined by anthropologist W.E.H. Stanner in his 1968 Boyer Lecture, *After the Dreaming*, articulated what he calls a 'cult of forgetfulness' where Australian history not only forgot but erased Aboriginal and Torres Strait Islander histories. Accounts of massacres, kidnappings and exclusion from all aspects of Australian life were ignored in education until about the 1970s and then, retold through white eyes. Aboriginal children sat in classrooms listening to tales of the savage or simple 'aborigine' who had nothing to contribute but was rather a burden on society – disposable if need be. Non-Aboriginal children had no other reference points to challenge these ideas that were often reinforced in the media.

The cumulative effect of decades of colonial education has contributed to the intergenerational trauma experienced by Aboriginal families, a form of epistemic and cultural genocide (Weuffen et al., 2023) from which there have been no reparations offered. This has enormous impacts on Aboriginal children as they progress through school, as well as fanning the flames of hostile relationships between Aboriginal and non-Aboriginal people.

Is it any wonder that teachers struggle with teaching Aboriginal children as well as teaching Aboriginal histories and cultures, as required by the Australian Curriculum's Aboriginal and Torres Strait Islander Cross Curriculum Priority (2022). Many teachers lack confidence due to their own poor education in this area and opportunities to build their knowledge and experience in this area (Burgess et al., 2022b). They fear offending Aboriginal students and their families by teaching the wrong information and/or being culturally inappropriate in the process (Captain & Burgess, 2022). The uncomfortable and controversial nature of many of the issues contribute to this fear – how do they incorporate this into their classrooms in ways that don't polarise debates or divide students? For some teachers it is a matter of not seeing the relevance as they don't teach Aboriginal students, ignorant of the fact that the Aboriginal Education Policy in NSW was deemed mandatory in 1987. And finally, as teachers grapple with an overcrowded, everchanging curriculum with constant demands from the media to also teach an exhaustive suite of life skills, teaching an area they are unfamiliar with is a step too far. This is not helped by limited support from curriculum and accreditation bodies who demand teachers to address Aboriginal education but provide little guidance of the 'how to' (Burgess & Lowe, 2022).

A teacher who made a difference

Teachers can make an enormous difference to the lives of their students, often not realising the impact they had until many years later. This is the story of authors, Kylie and Cathie. Kylie was that Aboriginal student who grew up in abject poverty with severe health conditions resulting in her missing a lot of school. By her teens, she was heading down a negative path of drug use and petty crime, believing that all she could hope to achieve was to get to the end of Year 10. Cathie was that teacher who believed Kylie was smart enough to go on to Year 11 and 12 and encouraged Kylie to join her Aboriginal Studies class. Kylie remembers the moment that changed her life. It was stepping into Cathie's classroom as a 16-year-old, and realising there was something special about her. Cathie had this incredible knack for making her feel valued and understood, 'She wasn't just teaching a curriculum but instilling a sense of pride and belonging in each of us'. This was the first time Kylie saw her family's story in the curriculum, and understanding this made her realise the power of education to change her life trajectory. Cathie remembers a shy girl with a hunger to learn about her history and culture. Kylie's effort and commitment to show up every day, despite the adversities she was facing and the gaps in her education, and to complete her senior studies was inspiring. Every teacher who has a student like Kylie is grateful they have chosen teaching as a career.

This story of our relationship spanning nearly three decades now sees us presenting highly successful professional learning for teachers and leaders based on our co-authored book 'Be that Teacher who Makes a Difference & Lead Aboriginal Education for all Students'. The main message of this book is to 'have a go', see Aboriginal children and their families through a strength-based rather than deficit lens, and believe all students can achieve.

Kylie now has her own business *Dream Big Education, Well being and Consulting* delivering messages of hope and optimism to Aboriginal students and community members, as well as teachers and leaders. While Kylie and

Cathie stand side by side as President and Vice President of the Aboriginal Studies Association, Kylie is now the teacher showing Cathie how to bring her expertise and passion to life, and running a successful business that allows her to do this work. The overwhelmingly positive feedback from masterclasses for teachers, leaders and Aboriginal community educators demonstrates that making a difference is as simple as believing in and supporting each other to listen to Aboriginal voices, 'have a go', and keep coming back.

Relationship building is central to what we do and who we are as teachers. Prioritising trust relationships with students facilitates calm and creative classrooms. Looking towards Aboriginal and Torres Strait Islander values of collectivity, reciprocity, and relationality can support this work. Classrooms that operate as a community of learners where ideas and knowledges are shared, and problems solved together, create a sense of belonging and a culturally safe space for all students to explore and challenge new and old ideas. Grounded in deep concern for humanity, this requires relational and holistic approaches for critical thinking and problem solving to think beyond the school gates. It also requires optimism and hope in taking courageous steps and making brave decisions.

What does the research tell us?

In 2019, 13 academics from 10 universities, conducted 10 systematic reviews analysing over 13,000 research studies from 2006 to 2017 (Guenther et al., 2019). These reviews covered key Indigenous Education topics in the areas of curriculum, pedagogy, leadership, professional learning, racism, literacy, numeracy, language and culture, community engagement, and remote education. Key findings across the reviews found that successful schools do the following:

- engage honestly and respectfully with parents and community
- demonstrate deep understanding of the local socio-cultural and political context resulting from colonisation
- focus on holistic, wraparound and culturally responsive strategies to support student, family, and community needs.
- articulate high expectations of students, teachers, and leaders.
- ensure curriculum, pedagogy and assessment reflects students' cultural backgrounds and interests, and is clearly scaffolded and supported.

- implement culture and language programs to build confident, engaged learners.

Localising curriculum and pedagogy

A Learning from Country Framework (LFC) has been developed by teacher educators and researchers Katrina Thorpe, Cathie Burgess, Suzanne Egan, and Valerie Harwood (Burgess et al., 2022a) to provide teachers with a guideline for embracing this challenging area and build confidence in their ability to do so. To understand this, we need to think about what we mean by Country when used in this context. Country is an Aboriginal English word that attempts to translate relational connections between Aboriginal people, place, and the non-human world (Thorpe et al., in press, pp. 1–2), as one Aboriginal community-based educator in the LFC project explains (Thorpe et al., in press, p. 129).

> I'm always learning even when I'm not by just looking at the environment because that's my big TV that's switched on even if I hadn't tuned in … this is my TV, my big billboard. You walk past down there, and it says, this is playing tonight. I just look at the trees and they're telling me what's happening. Everything's telling me what's happening.

This framework foregrounds Country as teacher. Its origins can be found in Tyson Yunkaporta and Aunty Doris Shillingsworth's relationally responsive standpoint (2020), which calls for a rethinking of the ways in which teaching and learning operates from the top down. Here, they flip the western approach of starting with doing something, by first understanding and reflecting on who we are, where we are and, on whose Country, and we do that by firstly applying First Nations Peoples' protocols and accountabilities. They describe this as follows:

1. The first step of Respect is aligned with values and protocols of introduction, setting rules and boundaries. This is the work of your spirit, your gut.
2. The second step, Connect, is about establishing strong relationships and routines of exchange that are equal for all involved. Your way of being is your way of relating because all things only exist in relationship to other things. This is the work of your heart.
3. The third step, Reflect, is about thinking as part of the group and collectively establishing a shared body of knowledge to inform what you will do. This is the work of the head.
4. The final step, Direct, is about acting on that shared knowledge in ways that are negotiated by all. This is the work of the hands. (pp. 11–12)

The LFC framework is very much grounded in the local, a place-based consciousness that informs curriculum content, teaching and learning strategies and building a sense of belonging for all students in the classroom. As Ruitenberg (2005) observes,

> Each place has a history, often a contested history, of the people who inhabited it in past times. Each place has as aesthetics, offers a sensory environment of sound, movement and image that is open to multiple interpretations. And each (inhabited) place has a spatial configuration through which power and other socio-politico-cultural mechanisms are at play. (p. 215)

The framework can be used by teachers to localise curriculum, develop culturally responsive pedagogical practices, build relationships for inclusive classrooms, engage with families and community and guide evidence of our teaching (Burgess et al., 2022b). The framework outlines four processes which, while appearing to be lineal, can be experienced in any order as we reflect on individual processes and how they collectively impact on our emotional, spiritual, cultural and cognitive engagement with LFC.

The first process, *Country-centred relationships*, focusses on listening to Aboriginal voices and thinking about Country as teacher. This being in and on Country, led by local Aboriginal knowledge holders and educators, not only includes the physical experience but the socio-cultural, historical, political and current issues embedded in the local community as a result of colonisation (Burgess et al., 2022b, p. 158). Walking with and deep listening to Aboriginal knowledge holders and educators requires cultural humility, an open heart and willingness to find strength in vulnerability to understand the significance of these knowledges to the children we teach, as well as to us as people living in a colonised land. Once you have begun this journey, you will be able to see and enact ways of bringing Country into the classroom, as well as exploring Country beyond the classroom door. This 'hands on' experiential approach to learning where answers are not the outcome, engages students through critical thinking, problem solving skills and an emotional investment in their own understanding of the place they live in.

The next process, *Relating* deepens these connections through truth telling, which includes listening to Aboriginal lived experiences of colonisation in this country. Engaging with uncomfortable and difficult knowledges can be distressing, even confronting, but when listening deeply, we start to build an understanding of the extent of the trauma resulting from colonisation and feel empathy for survivors and their message. Survivors often generously allay feelings of guilt and disempowerment as one preservice teacher noted

> I was astonished by the resilience of these survivors; somehow able to find the strength to talk about their trauma with patience, kindness and even humour – somehow, able to make the room laugh in between moments of tears and pain – a testament to their character and resilience.

Aboriginal speakers stress that while the past can't be changed, the future can, and once you have heard these accounts, you can't unhear them. For our preservice teachers experiencing this for the first time, they work through mixed emotions, to realise their opportunity to make a difference, as this preservice teacher reflected, 'It truly put everything into perspective that instead of focussing on shame from the past, I can use my position as an educator to truly have a positive impact on the future of many Aboriginal Peoples'. The survivors often talk about the healing power of these experiences and their sense of empowerment in educating future generations, a message that resonated with preservice teachers,

> The Uncles mention how sharing their stories is a way of healing, and they looked at us (future teachers) with hope and respect to create a culturally supportive environment that understands Aboriginal perspectives can break those cycles of intergenerational trauma.

This unexpected turn demonstrates the criticality of listening to build relationships between Aboriginal and non-Aboriginal people and generate healing for the common aim of ending the 'Great Australian Silence' and the intergenerational ignorance and racism still evident in society.

Critical engagement, the third process in the framework, occurs through reflection on the emotional and intellectual learning you have encountered through LFC experiences and prompts you to reflect on how this impacts personal and professional identity. This reflexivity enables you to position yourself as a learner rather than a teacher, embrace new ways of knowing, being and doing through an Aboriginal lens, and reimagine what an Aboriginal curriculum narrative might look like. The ability and willingness to engage in the process of conscientisation (Thorpe et al., 2021) reveals news ways of knowing, being, and doing through an Aboriginal lens, challenging western understandings of curriculum, pedagogy and schooling to activate a decolonising approach to education. As one preservice teacher keenly observes,

> The Uncles (survivors) demonstrated ways in which it might be possible to start deconstructing notions of teacher authority which are problematic for all students, but particularly Aboriginal and Torres Strait Islander students; demonstrating ways in which to decolonise the classroom.

The 'doing' occurs as you develop *culturally nourishing and sustaining teaching and learning practices* that engage all students and brings the school-community closer together. It involves sharing knowledges that direct actions, and creating culturally safe spaces for students to explore and critique what they are learning. As one preservice teacher explains,

> I hope to continue to learn and take this experience into my teaching practice, and to engage local Indigenous community members wherever possible to provide a culturally safe and diverse learning experience, not just for Indigenous students but for students of all cultural backgrounds in my classroom.

The 'doing' occurs throughout the LFC processes as you continue to think about how you will enact LFC in your classroom and maintain the relationships necessary to do this work.

The little things that make a difference

There are many small steps that can create a place of belonging for Aboriginal students and their families in schools. While some may argue that gestures such as flying the flag or putting up a few posters are tokenistic, they are only tokenistic if this is all you do. These actions can signal to families that you are interested in and supportive of their cultures and histories, but if this is all you do then they will see you as a 'tick-a-box' (Captain & Burgess, 2022) teacher only doing these things for your own career advancement. You need to go beyond these initial actions to demonstrate commitment and willingness to go the extra mile for their children and that you are willing to learn, unlearn and relearn (Captain & Burgess, 2022).

Aboriginal people are generally pleased when you ask for advice especially regarding issues of language, discourse and local community protocols. Language includes knowing what terminology is culturally appropriate for particular contexts. For example, 'part-Aboriginal' is an old term now considered offensive because of the way it was weaponised against Aboriginal people to remove children and deny identity. Discourse refers to the way in which Aboriginal peoples or cultures are talked about, for example, 'Close The

Gap'. While an important strategy, it frames Aboriginal people as 'less than', underachievers and a problem of their own making (Burgess & Lowe, 2022). Using the correct local protocols is important, for example Aunty and Uncle is often a term used as a mark of respect, usually (but not always) denoting Eldership. Getting these seemingly little things right makes a huge difference to Aboriginal people who see this as an indication of your level of respect and preparedness to listen (Captain & Burgess, 2022).

As the research mentioned above noted, those teachers and schools who genuinely engage with parents and communities are more likely to have success in their classrooms than those who don't. Creating opportunities for parents and community to provide advice and work with the school for positive events such as the schools' NAIDOC (a nationally recognised Aboriginal event) celebrations, makes a difference. Better still, those teachers who also participate in locally-run NAIDOC events (and other activities) will be seen as someone who is willing to go the extra mile.

Be brave – Turn up every day

There is no doubt that this is challenging work. As teachers, we represent the institution of education, an institution that could officially exclude Aboriginal children from schools up until 1972 (Captain & Burgess, 2022). Even if we don't realise it, we are seen as privileged and a beneficiary of the same colonisation that oppressed Aboriginal peoples. So we need to work harder and longer to gain trust to conceptualise what making a difference might look like. We must be prepared to be challenged about our role in perpetuating disadvantage, discrimination and antipathy – after all we are the educators who are in a position to break cycles of intergenerational ignorance and racism. This requires us to get out of our own way, set our egos aside and be vulnerable in a place we are normally in control of. But there is strength in vulnerability and good leaders will work from the shadows and sidelines to support others to shine and grow. This is what most teachers do, and do well, and do for the common good. Embracing the power of truth telling is essential if we are to create spaces for healing, not only for Aboriginal people, but for a colonial society that has yet to acknowledge and come to terms with its violent past and the ongoing impacts of this. If we can do this then we can make a, one child, one teacher and one school at a time, so that not another cohort of students will go through our system not knowing the true history of this country.

References

Australian Curriculum and Assessment and Reporting Authority. (2022). *Aboriginal and Torres Strait Islander histories and cultures*. https://v9.australiancurriculum.edu.au/downloads/cross-curriculum-priorities#accordion-00dfddc453-item-c84c8658c0

Burgess, C., & Lowe, K. (2022). Rhetoric vs reality: The disconnect between policy and practice for teachers implementing Aboriginal education in their schools. *Education Policy Analysis Archives, 30*(97). https://doi.org/10.14507/epaa.30.6175.

Burgess, C., Thorpe, K., Egan, S., & Harwood, V. (2022a). Towards a conceptual framework for Country-inspired teaching and learning *Teachers and Teaching*. https://doi.org/10.1080/13540602.2022.2137132

Burgess, C., Thorpe, K., Egan, S., & Harwood, V. (2022b). Learning from country to conceptualise what an Aboriginal curriculum narrative might look like in education. *Curriculum Perspectives, 42*(2), 157–169. https://doi.org/10.1007/s41297-022-00164-w

Captain, K., & Burgess, C. (2022). *Be that teacher who makes a difference and lead: Aboriginal education for all students*. Ultimate World Publishing

Guenther, J., Harrison, N., & Burgess, C. (2019). Editorial. Special issue. Aboriginal Vvices: Systematic reviews of Indigenous education. *The Australian Educational Researcher, 46*(2), 207–211.

Ruitenberg, C. (2005). Deconstructing the experience of the local: Toward a radical pedagogy of place. In K. Howe (Ed.), *Philosophy of education* (pp. 212–220). Philosophy Education Society.

Thorpe, K., Burgess, C., & Egan, S. (2021). Aboriginal community-led preservice teacher education: Learning from Country in the city. *Australian Journal of Teacher Education, 46*(1). https://ro.ecu.edu.au/ajte/vol46/iss1/4

Thorpe, K., Burgess, C. & Egan, S. (2024) *How teachers can use the Learning from Country Framework*. Centre for Professional Learning: NSW Teachers' Federation.

Weuffen, S., Lowe, K., & Burgess, C. (2023). Identity matters: Aboriginal educational sovereignty and futurity pushing back on the logic of elimination. *The Australian Educational Researcher. 50*, 1–10. https://doi.org/10.1007/s13384-023-00608-w

Yunkaporta, T., & Shillingsworth, D. (2020). Relationally responsive standpoint, *Journal of Indigenous Research, 8*(2020). https://doi.org/10.26077/ky71-qt27

HOPE AND COURAGE: A COLLECTIVE PEDAGOGY TO BUILD SUSTAINABLE GENDER EQUALITY AND MORE

Jane Hunter and Jorge Knijnik

Hope, courage, and wisdom in education is not in the province of schools alone. The essay that follows demonstrates our collective understanding of the ways in which sport and gender equality can work in the broader community to offer inspiration and learning for individuals, institutions, and the public good. Often, it's difficult to quantify and sustain momentum and change in schools, a mega sports phenomenon like the 2023 Fédération Internationale de Football Association (FIFA) Women's World Cup, offered optimism and a sense of collective achievement to young women who may otherwise have remained on the sporting sidelines. The vignette below takes the reader into a world perhaps they know little about but at its heart the goals of this international football event were not just about winning, entertainment and money – although such targets are certainly part of the story – there is much more to examine.

Vignette: A mysterious gender equality symposium

A few months before the 2023 FIFA Women's World Cup was held in Australia and New Zealand in July, Jorge, the second author of this paper, received an official invitation to attend a 'Gender Equality Symposium' in Brisbane, Australia. The invitation had the Australian Government logo, and it was signed by the 'FIFA Women's World Cup Taskforce of the Department of Foreign Affairs and Trade'.

The programme for the event detailed the presence of Australian politicians Senator Penny Wong, the Minister for Foreign Affairs, Senator Katy Gallagher, the Finance Minister and Minister for Women, and Anika Wells, the Minister for Aged Care and Sport, along with education and sports ministers from the Pacific Islands, Asia and Africa, and other dignitaries. Speakers included FIFA Secretary-General Fatma Samoura, the first women to have a seat in the premier tier of this major international sporting body, Football Australia executive members, Olympian and Paralympian athletes, First Nations star basketballer Patty Mills, and former Afghan women's football team captain Khalida Popal, who shared stories of survival, hope and courage in the face of the Taliban's tyranny.

Jorge's invitation was an acknowledgement of his more than 30 years of contributing to the field of sports, gender, and education, with a particular focus on women's football (Knijnik, 2013; Knijnik & Garton, 2022). He decided to attend.

After the Welcome to Country ceremony, Senator Wong addressed the audience. Her warm words to each country's representative were poignant. However, when it came to Nigeria, the final country she saluted, through gritted teeth she said: 'Welcome to the Nigerian Deputy High Commissioner'. In her all-green outfit, laughing and with open arms, Mrs Mercy Clement stood up. Her reaction was highly amusing as the Australians were still coming to terms with their beloved Matildas' (the Australia's women's football team) loss to the Super Falcons (the Nigerian women's football team) the previous day. The Matildas' chance of qualifying for the next phase of the tournament was in danger. Senator Wong retorted: 'No bad feelings, we have already forgotten this defeat and we will all move on!'

Soon after, the jovial mood in the symposium room changed when dozens of men in black suits entered the venue and stood against the walls. This was preparation for the arrival of Antony Blinken, United States Secretary of State, who then delivered a speech stressing how important football is to advancing the United Nations Sustainable Development Goal No 5 – gender equality.

Introduction to the essay

In this essay, we examine central concerns about women's football and the appropriation of gender equality by FIFA. Alongside this we ask whether the hopes about gender equality promoted during the Brisbane symposium were real or merely a 'sugar hit' designed to vanish as soon as the FIFA 'circus' left town.

We also posit that capitalism, as a social process, organises gender social relations in sport, particularly in football. We are particularly interested in whether the symposium on women's football during the 2023 FIFA World Cup was a questioning of the social order or an adjusting to the neoliberal status quo and how this major sporting event invaded the minds, discourses and practices of activists who had previously defended the community-based and anti-capitalist aspects of football.

Our first point of reference is consideration of how the United Nations regards gender equality as one of its 17 sustainable development goals (UNSDGs) (United Nations (UN), 2023). We then look at a previous study of hope and courage during a large international football event. Weaving in theoretical points about neoliberalism and pedagogical hope, we discuss data from the FIFA Women's World Cup *Legacy '23 Post-Tournament Report* (Football Australia, 2023) to see whether the event significantly advanced gender equality in Australia and beyond. In conclusion, we argue that a collective pedagogy of hope and courage can be built around women's football to advance not only gender equality but all the UNSDGs.

Gender equality and the United Nations

The UN's *Sustainable Development Goals Report 2023: Special Edition* (UN, 2023) calls for a rescue plan to achieve all 17 goals by 2030. Regardless of the global measure used for Goal 5, gender equality, targets for improving women's sexual and productive health rights and reducing discrimination and violence towards them are falling well short: a mere '15.4 per cent of gender equality indicators were "on track", 61.5% were at a moderate distance and 23.1% were far or very far off track from 2030 targets' (p. 23). The report also predicts that 'at the current rate, it will take an estimated 300 years to end child marriage ... 140 years for women to be represented equally in positions of leadership in the workplace, and 47 years to achieve equal representation in national parliaments' (p. 22). With less than six years remaining to achieve the goals, there are now only slightly more women in chambers of parliament, and legislated quota systems have led to women holding just 28.2% of management positions globally (p. 22). There is a fear that unless action is taken now, the 2030 UN agenda will become an epitaph for a world that might have been.

Football – 'The beautiful game'

Let's now step back a decade from our vignette to recall another mammoth FIFA event, the 2014 World Cup in Brazil. The authors of this essay (Knijnik

& Hunter, 2022) addressed notions of trust, humility, and courage in a paper that followed eight Aboriginal young people (five of whom are female) on a football tour from the remote Borroloola settlement in the Northern Territory (NT), Australia, all the way to Brazil. This tour was promoted by the John Moriarty Football (JMF) initiative. From data gathered in interviews with coaches and the youthful participants, and by using Freire's (2000) concepts of emancipation through dialogic practices, hope, critical consciousness, and untested feasibility, we examined the Borroloola youths' football educational activities as a dialogic space where autonomy and citizenship could be enhanced.

The stories told to us by the Borroloola participants demonstrated that beyond discourses of improving behaviours and educational outcomes, football as an educational activity can promote hope when participants embody the courage necessary to embrace it. Descriptions of 'joy' and 'happiness' during and after the football tour were common. When recalling their experiences, not only did the female players make many new friends, their interactions with Indigenous Brazilians also strengthened their own sense of cultural agency. John Moriarty told us, 'They were provided with uniforms, the JMF gear, and once they put that on, it transformed them – they are part of a team, and that's special' (Knijnik & Hunter, 2022, p. 379). He pointed out that the learning opportunities go beyond the sports themselves; they include literacy, dietary and health education. Upon returning to their community in the NT, many players embraced leadership roles and wanted to continue their football careers. This shows us how it's possible to achieve human transcendence when deliberate experiences built on notions of hope and courage act as instruments of community liberation (Freire, 2000).

In this essay we also draw on Nancy Fraser's (2017) concept of progressive neoliberalism and its pervasive influence on contemporary social practices. We examine how the mechanisms of capitalism may have co-opted football, transforming it from a potential instrument of community liberation into a vehicle for individual meritocracy.

Women's football and progressive neoliberalism

Capitalism extends beyond mere economics; it serves as a framework for organising both economic production and exchange and for influencing various non-economic relationships, activities and social processes that contribute to its functioning (Fraser, 2017). This comprehensive system shapes societal dynamics, resource allocations, and individual behaviours within the broader context of market-driven interactions. Fraser had witnessed what she termed 'progressive neoliberalism', a robust coalition between the 'modern sectors' of the economy, notably financial capital, and the emerging social movements advocating for the inclusion and equality of marginalised groups in society such as women, gender diverse communities, and racial minorities. Progressive neoliberalism ideologies are more focussed in the individual merits (meritocracy) of the so-called minorities than with realising fair outcomes (equality) for all. As a result, there has been a flourishing of identity politics without concomitant efforts towards economic redistribution. This focus on individual 'empowerment' rather than on structural changes has diminished the influence of economic struggles for resource control. Instead of advocating for economic resources, the efforts of most social movements have become entangled in a 'contest for recognition', thus limiting the expansion of alternative modes of living.

In the context of progressive neoliberalism, the popularity of women's football has grown exponentially. While this growth has undeniably been motivated by gender activists within the football context, it has also been co-opted by the markets and proponents of progressive neoliberalism to perpetuate unequal structures based on individual merits, rather than the achievement of sustainable change and equality. With this as backdrop, it is worthwhile re-examining Freire's (2000) ideas of hope and courage to see how they can guide us in overcoming the entanglements caused by progressive neoliberalism.

Freire, hope, and competitive sports

Freire (2000) posits that the displacement experienced during colonisation causes a sense of self-devaluation among colonised individuals and communities, which then lose the ability to articulate their knowledge and aspirations. Hence, they seek to not only assert their competencies and their intelligence but also produce them through their social efforts. Yet, they find themselves doubting their own capabilities.

Competitive sports have historically functioned as tools of colonial domination, and they have frequently been utilised by ruling political powers as cultural mechanisms to exert control over local populations (Knijnik & Garton, 2022). This corresponds with Freire's (2000) concept of 'cultural invasion' (p. 150), where the colonising group imposes its worldview and social practices on the invaded population, suppressing their creativity and genuine cultural expression. The actions undertaken by the oppressed reflect Freire's concept of a 'humanizing mission' (p. 200), an ongoing effort in which the oppressed, through communal courage and continuous dialogue fostering social awareness, strive to reveal the truths of cultural manipulation. Nevertheless, in regard to sports, oppressed communities do not passively accept colonisation; they actively resist the sports–colonial framework by challenging and disrupting the customs and interpretations imposed on their own sporting traditions by the enforcers of their coloniser's cultures and values (Knijnik, 2013; Knijnik & Garton, 2022). This relentless pursuit of human-isation inherently embodies hope and is capable of transforming individuals and communities involved in football – be they coaches, players, educators, or families – into catalysts for cultural change.

It is here where Freirean hope intersects with the criticism of progressive neoliberalism within women's football. Can the Freirean dialogue, as a social instrument for communal change, bring hope of improved living conditions and genuine equality for women in football communities?

The 2023 FIFA Women's World Cup: Advancing gender equality, or not?

In casual conversation with friends and family across Australia it's hard not to be drawn into discussions about the positive legacy of the 2023 Women's World Cup and the renewed interest in women's football. Often this is referred to as the 'Matildas effect'. For example, there has been a palpable increase in num-bers of dad's taking their daughters to games or to enrol in their local football clubs. In one state, in this case New South Wales (NSW) more than 25,000 young women have enrolled in football for the coming 2024 season. Data from the *Legacy '23 Post-Tournament Report* (Football Australia, 2023) are instructive. Using 'five pillars' – facilities; high performance; leadership and development; participation; and tourism and international engagement – it demonstrates how football can break down cultural barriers and foster under-standing of different peoples and cultures. In the words of Australia's Assistant Minister for Foreign Affairs, Tim Watts: 'This football tournament shows what can happen when you give women and girls the space to achieve' (p. 52).

Although the Matildas – the Australian women's football team – achieved fourth position overall in the tournament, it was the highest ever finish of a senior-level Australian football team. Two million people attended in person and there was a 'broadcast audience of 18.6 million with 70% of the Australian population tuning into football games over the two-week period – of which 56% were female audiences' (p. 62). During the event, six surveys targeted different Australian audiences, with a combined total of 6,707 responses received. In addition to the substantial increase in government investment, there were more than 150,000 new media articles, formidable merchandise sales, and huge levels of public participation. What is fascinating for the purposes of this essay is that the identified drivers of the impact of the Matildas are expressed as 'embodying modern Australian identity and values embracing integrity, female empowerment, diversity, resilience and teamwork' (p. 61). Linked to global influence and brand power, these achievements have placed Australian women's football on a hope trajectory – a 'future platform for good' (p. 63) – that includes the 2024 Paris Olympics, the 2027 FIFA Women's World Cup, and ultimately the 2032 Brisbane Olympics.

Football Australia (2023) makes eight claims about the impact of the Matildas' participation in the World Cup (p. 77). The event not only celebrated the achievements of female athletes but also augmented *gender inclusiveness and equality* by stimulating meaningful conversations and actions towards achieving gender parity in all facets of society (such as the Gender Equality Symposium mentioned earlier). By serving as a catalyst for engagement in sports and fostering a culture of fitness, it encouraged *increased physical activity and better health*. It enhanced *cultural inclusiveness and social cohesion* by embracing cultural diversity as a strength and creating a platform for cross-cultural exchange, thus showcasing the universal appeal of football and its capacity to promote harmony in an increasingly interconnected world. Through the shared passion for football, the tournament ignited positive *social and community behaviours* and a sense of belonging and camaraderie among spectators and participants alike, fostering a spirit of inclusivity and cooperation within local communities and beyond. Likewise, through the collective experience of witnessing remarkable athletic performances and engaging in the World Cup as a source of joy, inspiration, and emotional fulfillment, the *mental health and personal wellbeing* of individuals involved in it were improved. The sixth claim is related to *jobs and the economy*: the tournament generated a surge in economic activity, ranging from tourism and hospitality, positively influencing local business in a post-Covid period. It also reinforced the bonds of *national pride and identity* among Australians and nurtured Australia's *international reputation and diplomacy*, showcasing its status as a world-class destination for international competitions. For a sporting event that was only a month long, these outcomes are nothing short of remarkable.

Sugar hit or effective change?

While gender equality was the central theme of the Brisbane symposium mentioned in the opening vignette, attendees departed with a profound message from Senator Wong regarding the limitations of focussing solely on gender struggles in achieving the transformative goals outlined in the United Nations agenda. In her closing remarks, Wong reaffirmed Australia's commitment to the UNSDGs and emphasised their interconnectedness. For her, achieving gender equality is not feasible without addressing global issues such as hunger (SDG No. 2) and climate action (SDG No. 13), as these disproportionately affect women and girls. Wong also underscored the critical role of quality education (SDG No. 4) in tackling persistent inequalities in the job market and providing lifelong opportunities.

The symposium served as a touching moment of celebration, shattering entrenched stereotypes about gender and sports. Wong's words resonated deeply with the audience, prompting reflection on how the tools and momentum of events like the Women's World Cup might be leveraged to transcend gender equality and enact meaningful social change. Critics who dismissed women's matches as uninteresting and lacked excitement were proven wrong as stadiums overflowed and broadcast viewership soared. Such doubters were silenced by the thrilling intensity of the Matildas' penalty shootouts that captured the attention of Australia and the world. As well, the ensuing surge in membership packages for local women's football professional competitions has demonstrated a momentous shift in women's attitudes. The 2023 FIFA Women's World Cup was clearly more than just a fleeting 'sugar hit'.

Such events can serve as catalysts for broader social transformation, challenge ingrained biases and norms, and foster inclusivity and empowerment. The visibility and success of women's sports not only inspire future generations of athletes but also drive societal shifts towards gender equality. By harnessing the momentum they generate, advocates for gender equality can propel substantive change across various sectors, from education to employment to political representation.

Falling short ... the limitations of large sporting events

While the tournament symbolised progress towards gender equality in football, we must also acknowledge that it falls short of addressing the interconnected issues raised by the UNSDGs agenda, as mentioned by Senator Wong. At the end of the day, major sporting events are intrinsically connected to the neoliberal entertainment industry and their organisers tend not to question the economic purposes of this industry, lest they lose financial and political support.

It is imperative that we, as critical educators, look at the limitations of these large tournaments and address the issues surrounding them that remain unresolved, despite all the hype, energy, and investment. To create a framework for deconstructing their impact on societal transformation – in other words, a collective pedagogy rooted in hope and courage – we need to understand and apply Fraser's concept of progressive neoliberalism and Freire's critical pedagogy.

Fraser's analysis of progressive neoliberalism elucidates how ostensibly progressive agendas, such as gender equality in sports, can be co-opted by neoliberal capitalism, ultimately reinforcing systemic inequalities. While the Women's World Cup showcased the talent and athleticism of female athletes, it operated within a market-driven framework that commodified their labour and perpetuated economic disparities. For instance, while teams from the Global North (for example, Australia, United States, United Kingdom, Spain) had all the financial and structural support they needed to perform well on the field, national teams from the Global South (such as Jamaica and Nigeria) struggled to access the funds needed to support their wages and other necessities as high-performance athletes. Despite the temporary euphoria surrounding the tournament, such structural inequalities within the global sports industry remain largely unaddressed.

Given that the emphasis on individual meritocracy within the neoliberal paradigm undermines efforts to build solidarity and collective agency among marginalised communities, we can use Freire's critical pedagogy to emphasise the importance of conscientisation and collective action in challenging these sorts of situations. While the 2023 FIFA Women's World Cup may have inspired individual acts of empowerment and resistance, it did not catalyse a broader movement towards systemic change.

Furthermore, the commodification of women's sports within the neoliberal framework reinforces hierarchies of privilege and perpetuates exclusionary practices by putting rich and poor teams in opposition to each other and contrasting well-paid professional athletes to others who barely make the minimum needed for survival. Additionally, while the visibility of female athletes may challenge traditional gender norms, mainstream broadcasting risks essentialising notions of femininity and reinforcing narrow standards of beauty and athleticism. In this way, the Women's World Cup may inadvertently reproduce oppressive gender power dynamics rather than dismantling them.

A collective pedagogy based in hope and courage will entail transcending the commodification of sports and fostering genuine solidarity among athletes, fans, and advocates for social justice. By centring the voices and experiences of marginalised communities, we can challenge dominant narratives and envision alternative futures grounded in equality and inclusion.

We're hopeful and courageous but we're not there yet

While undoubtedly standing as a momentous event in the trajectory towards gender equality in sports, the impact of the 2023 FIFA Women's World Cup is singular and therefore insufficient for addressing the multifaceted challenges inherent in achieving comprehensive social change. However, as we celebrate the strides made in promoting gender equality within the sporting arena, it is essential to recognise that true progress will necessitate a broader integration of all the UNSDGs. By highlighting the talents and achievements of female athletes, the event intersects with those goals beyond gender equality. Senator Wong's touching remarks underscore the interconnectedness of these goals and the need to address them all collectively if Australia is to realise meaningful progress.

To truly advance the UNSDGs and build a collective pedagogy based in hope and courage, we must critically engage with underlying neoliberal systems of oppression and work towards dismantling them at their roots. Hence, the integration of all UNSDGs becomes paramount. By recognising the interconnectedness of social, economic, and environmental issues, we can develop more holistic approaches to addressing the underlying drivers of inequality and injustice. Achieving the collective goals that will benefit all members of society, particularly those who have been historically marginalised and excluded, will entail mobilising resources and fostering collaborations across communities.

In essence, while the 2023 FIFA Women's World Cup serves as a beacon of progress towards gender equality in sports, its significance lies in its potential to catalyse broader social change. By integrating the sustainability, equality and inclusion embodied in the UNSDGs, Freire's principles of pedagogical hope and courage, and Fraser's critique of progressive neoliberalism, we can harness the transformative power of sports to create a more just and equitable world for future generations.

References

Football Australia. (2023). *Legacy '23 post-tournament report.* https://www.footballaustralia.com.au/sites/ffa/files/2024-02/Legacy%20Post%20Tournament%20Report_A4_FA_%4096ppi_FINAL_22FEB2024.pdf

Fraser, N. (2017). Progressive neoliberalism versus reactionary populism: A Hobson's choice. In H. Geiselberger (Ed.), *The great regression* (pp. 40–48). Wiley.

Freire, P. (2000). *Pedagogy of the oppressed* (30th anniversary ed.). Continuum.

Knijnik, J. (2013). Visions of gender justice: Untested feasibility on the football fields of Brazil. *Journal of Sport and Social Issues, 37*(1), 8–30.

Knijnik, J., & Garton, G. (Eds.). (2022). *Women's football in Latin America: Social challenges and historical perspectives, Vol 2. Hispanic countries.* Springer Nature.

Knijnik, J., & Hunter, J. (2022). The pedagogy of courage: Critical Aboriginal football education in Australia's Northern Territory. *Critical Studies in Education, 63*(3), 371–386.

United Nations. (2023). *The sustainable development goals report.* https://unstats.un.org/sdgs/report/2023/

ROKEYA'S DREAM: SPECULATIVE WRITING AND THE MAKING OF AN UNREAL EDUCATION

Remy Low

Imagine

To begin, let us imagine a place where women move freely without fear, where the lives of human and non-human natures flourish side-by-side to their fullest potential. This is a place where the majority of each person's waking hours are spent in creative pursuits, where two hours spent at work is all that is required, where energy is drawn entirely from the heat of the sun to power machines that till the fields, and cars travel through the air using hydrogen propulsion. Water here is drawn from the atmosphere when needed and excess water is stored and rechannelled so that in the hottest, driest months, artificial fountains can cool the earth through regular showers. The religion of love for one another and commitment to truth governs social relations. And what establishes and drives this place to ever greater flourishing is education – an education system run entirely by and for women – and what secures it is not military force, but the value of its brain power, acknowledged by all.

Now let us imagine a space where women of different classes, castes, religions, races, ages, and abilities are welcomed. This is a space where education – in languages, mathematics, the arts, and vocational training – is offered freely to girls and women, many of whom have fled from situations of poverty, abuse, and neglect. In this space, women younger and older discuss and debate freely, each response to the other nourished by compassion, because each holds the other's story close to their heart. It is a space where staff and students care for one another's minds as well as bodies when they occasionally and inevitably become unwell. In this space, women learn from one another across the demographic lines that might otherwise divide them, connected by their common experiences of suffering in societies where the welfare and flourishing of women is inhibited. They are one in their resolve to challenge every inequity. This space will be their secure base.

That such a place and space sounds unreal to us is unsurprising given the very real facts we face: persistent gender injustices and educational inequities around the globe for those marked as female; pressures to narrow curricula at all levels of education to the efficient transfer of standardised, measurable, and marketable knowledge; frustrations, frayed tempers, and fractious relationships arising from overwork and underappreciation among those working in under-resourced educational institutions serving students with many needs; the simmering tensions of class, caste, religion, and race in societies structured by inequality; and the rapid degradation of environmental conditions that sustain human existence. We live in challenging times. And for those of us who have chosen to work as educators because we believe (or once believed) we could make a positive difference in the lives of others and, in that small but significant way, make the world slightly better, these times are experienced in our lives and bodies as stress. What, then, is the use of imagining such otherworldly places and spaces? Can the room that is opened between our presently stressful lived realities and the image of another less stressful reality offer hope? And how can such speculations help us to act with hope amidst oppressive circumstances and the stresses they induce?

In this essay, I will suggest that the exercise of imaginative powers, specifically in the practice of reading and writing speculative texts, is useful to us amidst the constant stream of stressors and helpful for making social change. I will advance this suggestion by offering a brief historical case study of the life context of the woman who conjured up the worlds I sketched at the beginning – Rokeya Sakhawat Hossain – and the difference she made. For if such utopian places and spaces might seem unreal to us, a quarter of the way through the 21st century and (as is likely to be the case if you are reading this chapter) from a society that affords a basic education to most, then consider how absurd these might appear in the context where they were penned: in early-20th century Bengal, ground zero of the British imperial subjugation of India, where colonial policies colluded with conservative communitarian tendencies to perpetuate gender, class, and caste inequalities, resulting in general literacy rates of under 10% and amongst women, hovering around 1%. But before turning to Rokeya[1] in that time and place, let us first turn to the impacts of chronic stress on our bodies and minds, and the potential for speculative writing to mitigate it.

Chronic stress and speculative writing

All of us who work in educational institutions are intimately familiar with stress. We can list amongst key stressors demands incumbent to the work of teaching – lesson preparation and delivery, timely marking and reporting, managing and caring for students' needs, collaborating with colleagues within and across disciplinary areas, communications with families and communities, and, of course, paperwork – to the unpredictable pressures that (inevitably) come up when internal or external circumstances impede the doing of one or more of the abovementioned tasks. The latter may include any number of contingencies that one might expect from an institution whose core business is the intellectual, social, and emotional development of a mass of students, each with unique proclivities, backstories, and home lives. External circumstances may also include the prevailing social and political currents of the day that, carried along in the minds and bodies of students and teachers, inevitably stream through the gates. All of this is not to mention the other stressors that may affect the lives of educators like health concerns, financial challenges, and the constant work of relationships. It is perhaps unsurprising that report after report finds stress to be pervasive amongst educators globally, and that stress-related conditions like depression, anxiety, and burnout register in significant numbers amongst teachers.

Stress, while useful in common parlance to signal that we are feeling under pressure, is quite a vague concept when subjected to scholarly analysis. Consider, for instance, what the commonalities are between the different things and events that we might label as 'stressful.' What is the relationship, say, between the stress of a looming deadline at work and the stress of an unpredictable home environment; or the stress of having to perform a task at work that we find temporarily unpleasant and the stress of having to perform an ongoing role in life that we find unbearable; or the stress of watching a *jump scare* horror film and the stress of constant vigilance against regular threats to our safety? Or, to bring in examples that may be more immediately relatable for those who work in educational institutions, what are the similarities or differences between periods of stress that are intrinsic to the job (e.g., marking, report writing) versus the stress of endemic workplace bullying and harassment?

Researchers in the field agree that there is no consensus in the scholarly literature as to the exact meaning of stress, with most defaulting to a classical view that stress is 'any challenge to the homeostasis [i.e., state of equilibrium in the bodily systems] of an individual that requires an adaptive response from that individual' (Sandi, 2013, p. 246), which can be used to refer to conditions ranging from mild challenges (e.g., deadlines, work tasks, horror films) to extremely aversive conditions (e.g., unpredictable home environment, unbearable life role, regular threats to safety). Fortunately, given the latitude of the concept, researchers have also classified and graded the different types of stressors that may be encountered and their stress effects on the body and mind (which I will denote as 'body-mind' because, pace Descartes, scholars across disciplines now largely agree are inextricably bound). Key parameters are the intensity of stressor, degree of perceived controllability and predictability of the stressful situation, and the frequency and/or duration of the stressor. Mild, controllable, predictable, and infrequent short-term stressors have been shown to enhance task-specific cognitive functions.

Chronic stress, especially when experienced as uncontrollable and/or unpredictable, appears to have less salutary effects. And it is this latter type that concerns us most in the present essay because of the nature of work facing many educators. So, while manageable acute stressors enhance our cognitive capacities to deal with the demands it imposes by temporarily arousing our bodies toward a narrowly focussed action orientation, the persistence of high stress, especially when perceived as unpredictable and uncontrollable, is associated with heightened anxiety and sensitivity to environmental threats, as well as depressive symptoms. Underlying all this is a functional reorganisation of our nervous systems, which adapt to chronic stress by prioritising what in the body-mind is regularly needed to cope (e.g., hypervigilance, withdrawal) and deprioritising what is not necessarily needed, like higher-order thinking (Sandi, 2013).

Among the many body-mind implications of chronic stress from the foregoing outline, plus many more that have not been mentioned (e.g., metabolic conditions, chronic pain), one consequence is worth highlighting with respect to the theme of this book: the decrease in cognitive flexibility and the corresponding increase in habitual behaviour. Does this mean chronic stress forecloses hope and the imaginative capacities that nourish it? What follows in this essay is an argument – perhaps a speculative one – that stress can be alleviated by the exercise of our capacity to imagine alternatives to our presently lived realities, specifically through the practice of reading and writing speculative texts.

The field of study that looks at how reading and writing fictional literature can affect the body-mind is at its infancy, although there are already interesting findings that suggest creative writing can improve some of the symptoms of chronic stress mentioned above (e.g., Pennebaker & Smyth, 2016). Making a specific case for body-mind value of speculative works in science fiction and fantasy, Esther L. Jones (2020) cites studies of how younger people's reading of such texts can help with living through chronically stressful times (e.g., the COVID pandemic), specifically by cultivating a 'dual empathy' through the worlds that such stories create. The process of dual empathy involves 'simultaneously engaging in intense personal processing of challenging issues, while "feeling through" characters, both of which produce benefits' (Jones, 2020). In addition to palliative benefits, she argues, writers of such speculative texts 'take an aspect of what is familiar and make it "odd" or "strange" enough to give the reader psychic and emotional distance to understand mental health issues with fresh eyes'; they also gift their readers 'an avenue to grapple with complexity and use their imagination to consider different ways of managing social challenges' (Jones, 2020).

Having detoured through a conceptualisation of chronic stress and its effects on the body-mind, and what speculative writing might offer as a way of responding to it, we are now at a good point to consider the exemplary life of Rokeya. What follows is a sketch of the life that she lived: the ground from which her writings arose to open up a psychic and emotional distance from the familiar, and the creative ways she took on the social challenges of her time and place. Through this cursory account of her life and work, we might come to an even deeper appreciation of her and the power of speculative writing for transforming oppressive, chronically stressful realities.

The places and spaces of Rokeya Hossain

In 1905, in the *Indian Ladies Magazine*, a short story entitled 'Sultana's Dream' appeared. Written by the 25-year-old Rokeya, it depicted a place – Ladyland – where for the sake of the wellbeing of all, it was decided that men should be confined to the home on account of the destructive wars they had unleashed.

In Ladyland, as sketched above in the first paragraph of this essay, women live in peace with one another and with nonhuman others, finding scientifically-driven ways to enable flourishing livelihoods in ways that do not also exact destructive costs on the environment. Education, not weapons or violence or exploitation, is the key to Ladyland's success.

It would not be an understatement to say that Ladyland was an inverted mirror image of the world Hossain inhabited. Born in 1880 into a rich zamindar (landowning) family in a village in the Rangpur district of British-ruled Bengal, Rokeya's life would be marked by what might today be called 'intersecting oppressions': she was subjected to the strictest form of purdah – where women are confined to specific and separate spaces within the home to conceal themselves from men and also unknown women – a practice prevalent in wealthier Muslim households and also some Hindu ones; treated with indifference by her parents likely owing to their contempt for a girl child as was the social norm at the time, she was denied any formal education and restricted in language learning to Urdu, which was regarded as the language of proper Muslims at the time since it was written in Arabic script unlike Bengali with its Sanskrit roots claimed by Hindu chauvinists, and English as the putatively anti-Islamic coloniser's language; and all this in a social context where Britain had been carrying out an imperial policy of degrading the status of Muslims and encouraging Hindu predominance to buttress their power (Quayum, 2017). To learn English – the language that 'Sultana's Dream' was written in – Rokeya had to take lessons from her sympathetic brother, Ibrahim Saber, under the cover of night 'after the parents and relatives, most importantly her father, had gone to bed' (Quayum, 2017, p. 6). When the time came for her to be married by her family in 1896 at the age of 16, it was also her brother who tactically recommended the 40-year-old widower Sakhawat Hossain, whom he knew to be generous and progressive, as a suitor. This was an arrangement that would provide the generative conditions for Rokeya's writing and work. Moving to Sakhawat's residence in Bhagalpur and away from the stifling conditions of her home of birth, Rokeya began publishing essays in various literary magazines, actively supported and championed by her husband (Quayum, 2017, p. 9). It was in this time that 'Sultana's Dream' was penned and published – all things considered, a remarkable and radical feat of imaginative upheaval of the world Rokeya knew.

As intimated above, one of the potentially useful functions of speculative writing in a utopian register may be that it taps into the human capacity to see alternatives, even under chronically stressful conditions, so that one might approach social challenges differently. Rather than strict blueprints for the future, then, speculative texts are thus best seen as creating mental openings where ideas for creative action can emerge. When Sakhawat passed away in 1909 leaving ₹10,000 to Rokeya for setting up a school for girls after his death, we can see how the psychic and emotional distance that opened up between Rokeya's reality and Ladyland of 'Sultana's Dream' created a space where Rokeya could act contrary to the world she had experienced. Beginning in Bhagalpur almost immediately after Sakhawat's death with a school of five students, Rokeya would subsequently relocate to Calcutta and establish Sakhawat Memorial Girls' School in March 1911 with an enrolment of eight; by 1915 there would be 84 students and in 1930, it would be extended to high school status with 10 grades and a wide-ranging curriculum including Qur'an recitation and exegesis, English, Bengali, Urdu, Persian, home nursing, first aid, cooking, and sewing (Quayum, 2017, pp. 10–13). While this may seem unremarkable to us, this was radically creative action for Rokeya on at least two counts: firstly, she had established an educational institution that was directly challenging the reality shaped by forces deeply invested in maintaining inequality along colonial, patriarchal, class, and caste lines; secondly, she had no clue how to run a school, having never been to one herself, and so had to courageously and actively seek wisdom from others about how to enact classroom teaching, school administration, and working effectively with community – particularly treading a path between sensitivity to customs like purdah while transforming archaic attitudes to girls' education (Quayum, 2017, pp. 11–12). According to Mohammad A. Quayum (2017), it was in pursuit of the latter, notably across communal lines, that she encountered other leading Bengali educationalists and feminists like Sarala Ray and Abala Bose and 'forged lifelong friendships with them' (pp. 11–12).

No doubt the twin tasks of running a school and refuting social censure – for which there was plenty – consumed much of Rokeya's time and energy. *Padmarag* (translated in English alternately as 'The Ruby' or 'Essence of the Lotus'), from where the space described in the second opening paragraph of this essay was drawn, was not published until 1924 – nearly two decades after 'Sultana's Dream'. Written in Bengali – the language of the masses in Bengal, yet another that Rokeya had to clandestinely learn in her youth against her parents' wishes, this time from her sister Karimunnesa Khanam Chaudhurani (Quayum, 2017, p. 4) – *Padmarag*, while not ostensibly speculative in the science fiction style of 'Sultana's Dream', is no less imaginative and utopian in the alternative reality it conjures. It is centred on a women-run educational and welfare institution where socially constructed lines of religion, race, class, and caste are cast aside for the sake of solidarity in opposition to patriarchal and colonial forces, and in pursuit of women's self-determination and flourishing. Unlike 'Sultana's Dream', *Padmarag* is laden with social realism. Notably cathartic for educators are chapters dedicated to describing teachers' work like reading letters of complaint from parents of students and frenetically preparing a prizegiving ceremony. Peppered throughout the novella are also character backstories of how women have transformed painful adversities in their lives through education and training to become key staff of Tarini Bhavan – the institutional space that the women inhabit. Inspiration for this novella was almost certainly drawn from her many years of running Sakhawat Memorial Girls' School, as well as the Anjuman-i-Khawatin-i-Islam (Muslim Women's Association) that she founded in 1916, which offered financial assistance to poor widows, provided shelter to physically and/or sexually abused wives, helped poor families marry off their daughters and, above all, ran literacy programmes among slum women, both Hindu and Muslim (Quayum, 2017, p. 16). While hovering closer to the reality that she lived, there are strong speculative elements in *Padmarag*. As Tanya Agathocleous (2022) notes in her introduction to a recent English edition of the text, these be seen in how 'Tarini Bhavan is a small island of utopian community within a real world of grossly unfair gender disparities', and in its determination throughout the narrative 'to flout expectations of genre and gender in order to show us both a deeply flawed world and people struggling to carve out a better one' (pp. xvii–xviii).

Taken together, both Ladyland of 'Sultana's Dream' and Tarini Bhavan of *Padmarag* present themselves to the reader as 'mental fortresses against pernicious gender ideologies and other conventional ideas' (Agathocleous, 2022, p. xviii). It is their utopianism, their very unreal quality, that a door to another possible reality than the one Rokeya lived in – and the one we live in – is opened.

Imagination as power

'Imagination,' according to Jean-Paul Sartre, 'is the whole of consciousness as it realizes its freedom' (Sartre, 1940/2004, p. 186). This is because for consciousness to be able to imagine, 'it must be able to escape from the world by its very nature, it must be able to stand back from the world by its own efforts' (Sartre, 1940/2004, p. 184). Imagination in his reckoning is thus no less than the power of consciousness to break free from the constraints of reality-as-it-is to bring forth an unreality – or better still, a 'not yet' reality.

Sartre's musings on the power of imagination were penned during his years as a high school teacher at the Lycée de Le Havre and published in 1940, just as Nazi Germany would take hold of most of France and install the authoritarian, anti-Semitic Vichy puppet regime to govern the remainder. By this time, Rokeya had been dead for nearly eight years, passing on in December 1932 at the age of 52. The French schoolteacher-philosopher would almost certainly not have known about the Bengali writer, educator, and feminist activist who lived nearly 8,000 kilometres away, doing her work also under the weight of oppressive forces. Yet had he read her writings and understood a little about the life she lived, I think he would have found a manifestation of his theory on the power of imagination: an 'apprehension of the real [that] implies a hidden surpassing towards the imaginary' (Sartre, 2004/1940, p. 188). This surpassing is an act of freedom even in oppressive, chronically stressful situations – the power to imagine things being otherwise so that in the space opened up between the real and imagined, our next steps may be toward the latter. That Rokeya's school still stands today educating more than 1,200 girls each day, that we might still be reading 'Sultana's Dream' and *Padmarag* seeking visions of better places and spaces, is a testament to the power of her imagination to conjure up an unreal world and her courage to walk towards it.

In our own difficult times, may we too find the power to exercise our imaginative capacities to articulate alternatives to the reality we live in, and the courage to take steps in the direction of those alternatives. And may the story of Rokeya Hossain's life and work offer us hope as we do so.

Note

1 In accordance with Bengali language convention and to avoid confusion further below when referring to family members (i.e., husband), I will refer to Bengali individuals by their given name (what in English language convention is called "first name"). So, "Rokeya" rather than "Hossain."

References

Agathocleous, T. (2022). Introduction. In R. Hossain, *Sultana's dream and Padmarag* (B. Bagchi, Trans., pp. vii–xviii). Penguin.

Jones, E. (2020, May 11). Science fiction builds mental resiliency in young readers. *The Conversation.* https://theconversation.com/science-fiction-builds-mental-resiliency-in-young-readers-135513

Pennebaker, J. W., & Smyth, J. M. (2016). *Opening up by writing it down: How expressive writing improves health and eases emotional pain.* Guilford Publications.

Quayum, M. A. (2017). Rokeya Sakhawat Hossain: A biographical essay. In M. A. Quayum & M. M. Hasan (Eds.), *A feminist foremother: Critical essays on Rokeya Sakhawat Hossain* (pp. 1–23). Orient Blackswan.

Sandi, C. (2013). Stress and cognition. *Wiley Interdisciplinary Reviews: Cognitive Science, 4*(3), 245–261.

Sartre, J. P. (2004). *The imaginary: A phenomenological psychology of the imagination.* Routledge. (Original work published in 1940)

THE INCREDIBLE LIGHTNESS OF TEACHER PROFESSIONAL BEING: HOPE, COURAGE AND WISDOM IN THE WORK OF SCHOOLS AND TEACHERS

An Afterword

Bob Lingard

Practice living in a policy world

By way of introduction to this essay, written as an 'afterword', I will very briefly summarise the structural and policy conditions that teachers now work under so as to reinforce the necessity of hope, courage and wisdom in teachers' professional dispositions and in the individual and collective and collaborative practices of teachers and schools. Corporate managerialism has been the way of state restructuring in education over the last three decades as a complement to the broader frames of neoliberalism, which prioritise the market over the state and the possessive individual over the common good. In this way the state devolves responsibility, indentured autonomy, for achieving central goals to schools. Today, while systems still have high level goals these are often simple rearticulated in practice as test results. What we have are reductive test-based and top-down modes of accountability with real impact on pedagogies, the enacted curriculum and on broader teacher professional practices. The concept of socially just schooling is thinned out and expressed only in statistical terms. A retethering is required.

Of course, these effects play out differently in schools positioned differently in the social structure, with the most unjust impacts on the work of teachers toiling in schools in the poorest communities, who are subject to the harshest panoptic gaze of top-down, test-based accountability. I am reminded here of a number of teachers working in an elite, very successful all-girls school in the United Kingdom, who had all worked for considerable periods of time in the government sector, and who told me the reason they were now at this school was that they could at last be the teachers they had always wanted to be; an unsaid acknowledgment of the hope, and courage central to teaching, particularly so for teaching in schools in poor communities, and also of the impact of unequal structures of schooling on the work of teachers. They were also probably referencing the lifting of top-down policy pressures and acknowledging the impact of poverty on teachers' work, while recognising the privileged teaching positions they now held, as well as the privilege of the student body and the girls' assured optimism and capacity to aspire regarding their university and professional futures. Certainly, the Head of the school made these acknowledgments to me. I was in the school for a prolonged period as part of a research project using Bourdieu to understand the reproduction of privilege. Interestingly, the Head asked me to address a full school assembly to explain to the students the project and Bourdieu's theorising about capitals, indicative of the school's autonomy and liberal education approach.

We also know that inequality has grown in all advanced nations since the onslaught of neoliberalism. This has significantly affected the work of schools in poor communities and made it more challenging to ensure that all students irrespective of their backgrounds have this capacity to aspire. This has had significant effect on the work of teachers in schools serving the poorest communities.

As Bernstein noted a longtime ago, the three central message systems of schooling (curriculum, pedagogy and evaluation) sit in a symbiotic relationship with each other; changes in one affect the others. Today high-stakes testing provides the dominant message system with real effects on curriculum and pedagogy, the central defining elements of the work of teachers. Pedagogy is how schooling gets done, while curriculum is what gets done. This mode of accountability has, as already noted, differential class-based effects on schools.

In the contemporary Australian education policy context, there is deeply unequal and unjust funding of schools (nearly all government schools are funded below the government's own benchmark, the School Resource Standard, while all non-government schools are funded above the standard). In effect we have a redistribution of funding to the better off schools and students: a deep injustice. I would suggest this constitutes a disaffecting hidden curriculum to the work of schools and teachers. It is a sad reality that the teacher unions, the collective voice of teachers, work assiduously to challenge and overcome.

More broadly, contemporary education policy takes on a one-size-fits-all approach with an explicit denial of teachers' professional judgment. The centrality of professional judgment means we can only ever have evidence-informed practice, not evidence-based, which policymakers speak of *ad nauseum*. We see the proclivity of contemporary education policy for a one-size-fits-all approach, for example, in the exhortation by several school systems in Australia for teachers to adopt direct instruction as the gold standard pedagogy, again denying the complexities of pedagogy in respect of different topics, students and also the necessity of enabling teacher professional judgment. Recent policy moves and imperatives in Australia regarding teacher education also insist on a one-size-fits all approach. Private sector companies such as McKinsey proffer policy advice to school systems and this is given greater salience by policy makers than academic research. As a result such work seeks to enhance its impact by proffering a one-size-fits-all approach to systemic reform. Think of McKinsey's (2007) *How the world's best-performing school systems come out on top* and its global influence. Its recent (2024) report, *Spark & Sustain: How all the world's school systems can improve learning at scale*, will likely have similar impact. Such a perspective denies the significance of educational research and the professional knowledge of teachers and school leaders.

In the macro policy context of neoliberalism and new managerialism, there has been enhanced involvement of private sector actors, particularly edu-businesses and edtech companies, in education policy processes and in the work of school systems (e.g., student management systems; data infrastructures; test management) and the work of schools and teachers (commercial curricula and materials; tests; professional development). One-line budgets and thinned out systemic supports sees schools purchasing commercial materials and services to assist schools in managing increased workloads and work intensification and teachers' 'time poverty'. While the purchase of commercial curricula and curriculum materials, along with lesson plans, is supposed to lessen teacher workloads, it also deprofessionalises teachers, as curriculum work is central to teacher professional practices.

I have mentioned teachers as curriculum workers; they enact the intended curriculum. Schooling also gets done through pedagogy. More specifically, teachers do schooling through their pedagogical content knowledge. This is where the expert teacher brings together their knowledge of how to teach with their subject knowledge, along with knowledge of their students and school context. Despite all of the multifarious, reductive, controlling policy, accountability and evaluation pressures that seek to delimit teacher professional autonomy in contemporary schooling systems, I would argue that teachers still retain some real control over pedagogical content knowledge. This is the core element of teacher professionalism, where teachers enact courage and wisdom interwoven with an ethics of hope and democratic desires and aspirations for a better world. I would aver that hope is perched in the soul of teachers.

Evidencing hope, courage and wisdom

Teachers, students, researchers and communities

I will report here in this vignette on a large research council-funded research project in which our research team worked very closely with eight schools and teachers in disadvantaged communities in rural Queensland over three years to help teachers, students and their communities create an alternative, more educative bottom-up mode of accountability that challenged the extant and restrictive dominant top-down, test-based approach (see Lingard et al., 2021 for full details). In the first stage, the research team worked collaboratively with stakeholders to develop case studies of eight schools, which outlined the negative impact of existing accountabilities in these schools. We documented very deep concern amongst both teachers and principals about the restricted and limiting nature of the empirical data to which they were held to account and what they saw as the anti-educative effects of this test-based mode. They wanted an expanded mode of accountability linked to the broadest goals of schooling and also desired accountability to function in multiple directions: for example, between the schools and their communities, functioning from both schools to their communities and from the communities to the schools in a horizontal fashion; also they wanted an additional vertical form of accountability, holding policy makers and the system to account in addition to the current, vertical top-down panoptic gaze. The schools were happy to be held to account, for the broader purposes of schooling, not just test results, but they also wanted to be able to give accounts of their achievements, including narratives not just data. Research conversations with the teacher unions also confirmed their support for such an approach.

Stage Two saw workshops provided by the research team to support teachers to design and implement rich approaches to teaching, learning and assessment as part of community focussed and located History curriculum units in lower secondary schooling. Student-researchers helped to identify resources that could be used to connect school learning with the needs and aspirations of the communities the schools served. The findings from student research projects, as well as students' and teachers' experiences of working with community members and community knowledges, funds of knowledge, in curricular ways, were included as one important set of rich accounts that were subsequently gathered by the *Learning Commission*.

We created and convened a *Learning Commission* in Stage Three, chaired by a retired local school principal, which comprised community members to inquire into what communities in the area expected of schools, what resources were required to meet these expectations, and how communities would know if their expectations were being met. Membership included a local politician, a local journalist, a representative of Indigenous communities, representatives from local businesses and community groups, and a representative from the state department of education. The curated *Learning Commission* conversations were to contribute to conceptualising a different and more educative mode of accountability. As such, the *Learning Commission* process expanded the conversation about how schools could develop rich accounts of their achievements, including contributions from a broader cross-section of community members. Submissions were made to the *Learning Commission* by the teachers and students involved in the second stage of the project, as well as from principals and a broad range of community groups.

In the final stage, researchers along with principals, teachers, students and community and local politicians and senior state department of education officials held a public meeting towards conceptualising the new mode of accountability, drawing on a presentation of all the evidence collected to that point. Subsequently, these groups, led by the researchers, attempted to synthesise the data collected across all four stages, and in the fifth and final stage we collaboratively conceptualised a concept of rich accountabilities that involved interrogating and translating the understandings derived from the other stages, particularly the contributions and insights of the *Learning Commission*.

The point of this vignette has been to illustrate how a Director-General of Education, a former successful school principal, had the courage, and indeed wisdom, to allow this research project to be conducted in Queensland schools to challenge hegemonic policies, the dominant mode of accountability and allowed and facilitated schools and their communities to articulate and justify their concerns about these, as well as putting forward alternatives. This project was extremely well received in the schools, amongst the principals, the teachers, students and by their communities. Indeed, the local newspaper ran a very positive story about the positives of the project and the flourishing of hope in these schools, their classrooms and their communities. Parents were also very positive. This collaborative and democratic project, bringing together research knowledge, professional knowledge and community funds of knowledge enabled teacher professional judgement and mobilised resources of hope in the school and in communities and produced an effective rich mode of accountability. This had real impact on these schools and their work, and on teachers, students and school and community leaders and on systemic policies. We also witnessed the strong commitments of all involved in the project to the necessary and intimate imbrications of schooling and democracy.

Parent and teacher activism in New York State

This case deals, albeit briefly, with parent and teacher activism in New York state in opposition to the federal and state policy moves to high stakes testing for all students in Grades 3 through 8 in maths and language arts, and related evaluation and accountability of teachers, following G.W. Bush's implementation of the bipartisan *No Child Left Behind Act* in 2002 and developed further under President Obama's *Race to the Top* legislation, 2009. Subsequently, the tests were linked to the Common Core State Standards for curriculum with a stress on Adequate Yearly Progress. There was in New York State in the early part of this century almost consensus across Democratic and Republican lines for these developments, along with the establishment of systemic data infrastructures, and the involvement of philanthropies and edu-businesses in policy and the work of schools; the creation of publicly funded, but privately managed Charter Schools being a good case in point. *Race to the Top* offered competitively allocated extra federal funds to the cash-strapped states in return for adoption of a raft of schooling reforms, including common standards and tests, test-based teacher evaluations, expansion of Charter Schools, and the creation of data systems and infrastructures.

In a research project, funded by the New South Wales Teachers Federation, the largest teacher union in Australia and with support from Education International, the international federation of teacher unions, with Rochester University colleague, David Hursh, we researched the opposition to these policy developments through a focus on two Activist parent groups, Long Island Opt-Out (LIOO) and New York State Allies for Public Education (NYSAPE), as well as researching activist teachers, school principals and union members (Lingard & Hursh, 2019).

The initial focus of both groups was to encourage large numbers of parents to opt their children out of the tests. In this, they were amazingly successful and being so successful they challenged the validity of the collected test data for use in policy and for accountability and teacher evaluation purposes. In our research, we documented how these groups rejected a construction of them in neo-liberal market terms as simply consumers (parents) and implementers (teachers) of government policies. On the latter, many of the members of both groups were activist teachers and many activist school principals were also involved. About 50% of the membership of opt-out groups were actually activist teachers. The membership was also highly educated, largely but not exclusively white, and with high incomes. The teachers got involved because policy makers were not listening to their complaints and because the teacher unions had some ambivalence about the opt-out movement, especially in respect of Obama's civil rights framing of *Race to the Top*. Some teacher dissatisfaction with the teacher union stance resulted in the creation of other pressure groups such as the Badass Teachers Association.

All involved with opt-out (parents, community members, teachers) perceived themselves as democratic citizens with a right to participate in democratic conversations about education policy. These groups developed a 21st century mode of social media activism, which worked in horizontal ways linked to communities. They used this community-based, techno-savvy mode of activism to then pressure policy makers for change. and to encourage parents to opt-out of the standardised tests. They were very active on social media with an informative Webpage and regular well attended public forums across the state. There were also public demonstrations; opt-out was an effective 21st century social movement.

Elsewhere, David Hursh and his colleagues (2020), including the leaders of the two opt-out groups, have documented the work of parent activism and teacher involvement. Teacher involvement in opt-out provided the professional and substantial knowledge base of the movement. No 'teacher bashing' was a central motif of the movement. Its focus was in the first instance local, but also targeted state and federal policy frameworks and agendas aligned with standardised testing and the privatisation of schooling.

This activist politics was very successful in getting parents to have their children opt-out of the test; for example, with 20% of students opting out of the federally mandated tests in 2015 and 22% in 2016, with more than 50% opting out on Long Island. The extent of this opting out seriously challenged the reliability and validity of the test and as a consequence challenged the legitimacy of its use for teacher revaluation purposes. This was a goal of the opt-out movement and of the activist teachers.

Democracy in a primary school

In a government funded research project I conducted with a large team some time ago, we witnessed (student) democracy at work in a few schools; this was not simply learning *about* democracy, but also in a prefigurative way learning *through* democracy *for* democracy (see Leach et al., 2023). The goal was producing active and informed (local, national and global) citizens. In the exemplary democratic primary school, the teachers framed in the first instance the structure, goals and practices of student democracy, but once established and working, students took full control. Each class had a democratic student committee with articulated functions. There was also a whole school democratically elected committee. Each was chaired by an elected student. There were also elected agenda committees. Teachers acted as advisors. The whole school committee agreed on voted-for recommendations for changes and improvements that the chair then sent to and represented to the school's governing council. The school council, principal and teachers took all recommended changes and advice from the various elected student committees very seriously. Students raised matters of school resources, school, classroom, and playground design and facilities, timetabling issues, educational matters, raising money for disadvantaged groups, global matters to do with the climate emergency and sustainability, including recycling, school landscaping and so on. This democratic work cut across so many curriculum areas: language, science, maths, and social studies. Issues could be raised by any student or group of students to be considered by the relevant committee. Teachers commented on how these practices built a real sense of school community and ownership and commitment of students to their learning and to their school, but also to broader communities: enacting active and informed local, national and global citizenship in a progressive and prefigurative way. These practices instantiated hope in the work of the students, teachers and the school and evidenced the courage and wisdom of the teachers and principal in seeking to build a better future through encouraging a democratic role for students in the work of the school.

Impacts of teaching

This piece of evidence relates to my wife as a teacher of ancient and modern history and a leader in schools for 48 years. I offer this case to stress the significance, both short and long term, of teachers' pedagogical content knowledge; what I see as a core element of teacher professionalism and at its very best, enfolded by and expressing hope, courage and wisdom.

In 2023, the Queensland Murdoch daily newspaper, *The Courier-Mail*, ran a feature asking all state politicians about the formative impacts on them of their schooling and of teachers. The Greens member for South Brisbane in the state parliament in her observations waxed lyrical about the significant long-term effects and impacts of my wife's teaching her senior ancient and modern history. She asserted that how she was taught (pedagogical content knowledge) these subjects by my wife had developed her capacity for finding, using, analysing and evaluating evidence in a critical and open way and that while this was done in subject history, she argued these skills had broader long-term significance for her adult life. After school she had completed an Honours degree and then a PhD in sociology and was now an elected Greens member of parliament, who had defeated the former Deputy Premier in the state election. She implied the centrality of her learning in senior schooling history subjects not only to her subsequent educational and career trajectories, but also to her actual being in the world, her human dispositions, and to the capacity to aspire to a better more sustainable world

Closing

Susan Groundwater-Smith's opening and the essays in this collection provide something of an archive of the actuality and potential for hope, courage and wisdom in progressive teacher professionalism and more broadly in the educative and democratic work of schools. I am thinking here of the archive in

Derrida's (1998) sense as being constitutive; here constitutive of a desired and necessary teacher professionalism, its incredible lightness of being, which seeks in so many ways to challenge and limit the impacts of the reductive contemporary policy frames considered above. As such, the collection creates a significant resource for hope against the heavy weight of the contemporary world and contemporary education systems and limiting anaemic policy frames. This afterword essay has sought to demonstrate instances of such hope, courage and wisdom in the individual and collective pedagogical and curriculum work of teachers.

UNESCO's recent report (2021), *Reimagining our futures together: A new social contract for education* also provides such a resource; a resource to be utilised by teachers, their unions and professional associations to challenge the privatisation and economisation of contemporary education policy, individually and collectively. This report argues, correctly in my view that:

> Our humanity and Planet Earth are under threat. The pandemic has only served to prove our fragility and interconnectedness. Now urgent action, taken together, is needed to change course, and reimagine our futures.

The report sustains a strong case of the pressing need for a new social contract to frame education policy and practice; one that will 'repair injustices', while 'transforming the future' through the work of policy, schools and teachers. The report also argues the necessity of schools creating prefigurative realities of a sustainable and carbon neutral democratic and socially just future. The report notes: 'In a new social contract for education, pedagogy should be rooted in cooperation and solidarity, building the capacities of students and teachers to work together in trust to transform the world'. *Reimagining our futures together* provides resources for hope for individual teachers, but also for their collective voices through their unions and professional associations.

In Appadurai's (2013, p. 295) words, as with this collection, the report provides an ethics of possibilities, where professional and community conversations can aspire to creating a better world and better schooling for all. This would challenge the dominant contemporary trope of an ethics of probabilities, where big data, numbers, algorithms, dataveillance, machine cognition and potentially AI, together drive a future with limited human interventions and aspirations. The resources of hope challenge this dystopian future and argue the necessity of human judgement and cognition to work with machine cognition, but with latter being emptied of the 'arbitrary, discriminatory and, certainly, biased cultural codes' (Airoldi, 2022, pp. 154–155) that currently ensure the reproduction of inequalities through schooling and correlated reproduction of an unjust society. Teacher pedagogical content knowledge, pedagogies of hope, courage and wisdom, individually and collectively, can challenge this situation in both small and large ways and must do so in prefigurative ways to help usher in a better future at a moment when unfortunately hope and history do not rhyme. The incredible lightness of the teacher professional being means we only get one chance to instantiate the necessary hope, courage and wisdom in practice to challenge the heavy weight of the contemporary world and of debilitating systemic education policies.

References

Airoldi, M. (2022). *Machine habitus: Toward a sociology of algorithms*. Polity.

Appadurai, A. (2013). *The future as cultural fact: Essays on the global condition*. London: Verso.

Derrida, J. (1998). *Archive fever: A Freudian impression*. Chicago University Press

Hursh, D., Deutermann, J., Rudley, L., Chen, Z., & McGinnis, S. (2020). *Opting out: The story of the parents' grassroots movement to achieve whole-child public schools*. Myers Education Press.

Leach, T., Collet-Sabe, J., Bardolet, A. T., Gil, N. S., & Clarke, M. (2023). The role of education in democracy: Continuing the debate. *Oxford Review of Education*, 50(4), 484–498.

Lingard, B., Baroutsis, A., & Sellar, S. (2021). Enriching educational accountabilities through collaborative public conversations: Conceptual and methodological insights from the *Learning Commission* approach. *Journal of Educational Change*, 22(4), 565–587.

Lingard, B., & Hursh, D. (2019). Grassroots democracy in New York state: Opting out and resisting the corporate reform agenda in schooling. In S. Riddle & M. W. Apple (Eds.), *Re-imagining democracy for education* (pp. 239–255). Routledge

McKinsey & Company (2007). *How the world's best performing schools come out on top*. September

United Nations Educational Scientific and Cultural Organisaition. (2021). *Reimagining our futures together: A new social contract for education*. UNESCO.

CONSOLIDATED BIOS

CATHIE BURGESS is an Associate Professor leading teaching/research projects in Learning from Country, Leadership in Aboriginal Education and Culturally Nourishing Schooling at the Sydney School of Education and Social Work, The University of Sydney. She has extensive teaching and leadership experience in secondary schools and maintains strong connections with school-communities. Along with extensive academic publications, Cathie has co-authored best-selling book 'Be that Teacher Who Makes a Difference' with Kylie Captain and delivers transformative professional learning to bring the book to life. Cathie's work in Aboriginal Education/Aboriginal Studies is acknowledged through an Honorary Life Member, NSW Aboriginal Education Consultative Group and Life Member, Aboriginal Studies Association NSW.

CATHERINE BURKE is Emerita Professor of the History of Education at the University of Cambridge, UK. Her research examines the relationship between innovation in teaching and the design of formal and informal learning environments; the view of the child and young person in the design of education; the history of 20th century school architecture and its pioneers. She has published on the history of school architecture, the participation of children in the design of school, as well as on contemporary school architecture. She is currently, with Professor Jane Martin of the University of Birmingham, joint series editor of the Routledge Progressive Education series.

KYLIE CAPTAIN is a proud Gamilaroi woman author and educator with a passion for inspiring positive change and empowerment. Her bestselling books and journals are making a difference in the lives of countless individuals across Australia and abroad. As the Founding Director of Dream Big Education Wellbeing & Education and President of the Aboriginal Studies Association, Kylie brings over two decades of expertise in Aboriginal education, child protection and community services. *Kylie is passionate about utilising her experiences and adversities to make a difference in the lives of many – one student, school and organisation at a time.*

BARRY DOWN Barry Down is Adjunct Professor, University of South Australia and Emeritus Professor, Murdoch University, Western Australia. His research has focussed on teacher's work, student engagement, voiced research, and socially just school reform. Barry has co-authored and edited many books (with long time collaborators John Smyth and Peter McInerney) including *Critically Engaged Learning; Activist and socially critical school and community renewal; Hanging in with kids' in tough times; Critical voices in teacher education; The socially just school; Doing critical educational research* (with Rob Hattam); *Rethinking school-to-work transitions* (with Janean Robinson); and *The sage handbook of critical pedagogies* (with Shirley Steinberg). His current research investigates the impact of school exclusions on the lives of marginalised students and their families.

SUSAN GROUNDWATER-SMITH Susan Groundwater-Smith (AM) is an Honorary Professor in the Sydney School of Education and Social Work. Her published and practical work, over many years has been directed towards teacher professional learning through engagement with action research. More recently, she has focussed upon the generative possibilities that arise from consulting with and decision sharing with young people regarding the ways in which educational practices impact upon them, both within schools and cultural institutions. As well as professorial positions in Australia she has held university appointments in UK and the Netherlands.

JANE HUNTER Jane Hunter is a former teacher. She is an Associate Professor in teacher education specialising in curriculum, pedagogy, and digital learning in K-12 education at the University of Technology Sydney, Australia. Her work reinforces the importance of continuous teacher professional learning through ongoing school-university partnerships. Jane's research with teachers known as 'High Possibility Classrooms' was awarded 'high impact' by the Australian Research Council (2019); her latest book featuring research on integrated STEM with teachers recommends a new 'blueprint' for Australian schools; she tweets @janehunter01.Her new venture is a podcast series Talking Teachers that offers solutions to the current challenges in our schools.

STEPHEN KEMMIS Stephen Kemmis is Professor Emeritus of Federation University, and of Charles Sturt University, Australia. He studies the nature and change of practices, principally in education, through the lens of the theory of practice architectures. He writes on education, critical participatory action research, higher education development, approaches to research, and Indigenous education. He is co-founder of the Pedagogy, Education and Praxis international research network including researchers from Australia, Finland, the Netherlands, New Zealand, Norway, Sweden, Colombia, and the Caribbean. He has held university appointments in Australia, the USA, and the UK, and has been a visiting scholar at various universities internationally.

JORGE KNIJNIK Jorge Knijnik is an Associate Professor in the School of Education and a researcher in the Centre for Educational Research at Western Sydney University, Australia. He is an inaugural committee member of Women in Football Australia, a national association whose mission is to support gender equity within the Australian sports context. His task on this board is to create a research philosophy among all sport participants – communities, NGOs, players, industry, and football bodies – thus endorsing an ethos of evidence-based decision making in the arena of sports, education, and gender equity. Jorge has numerous scholarly publications; he tweets @JorgeKni

BOB LINGARD is Emeritus Professor in the School of Education, The University of Queensland. Among many other honours he is a Fellow of the Academy of Social Sciences in both Australia and UK. He has authored many books and chapters focussing on educational policy making at the local and global levels;

in particular paying attention to issues in relation to social equity. He has held international professorial appointments in England and Scotland. Over the years he has mentored both academic colleagues and practitioners in the field and in many cases co-authored publications with them.

REMY LOW Remy Low is committed to cultivating culturally responsive educators who can work in diverse contexts. This informs his research, which flows in two broad directions. First, he examines the social and cultural forces that have shaped education in the present. Second, he explores practices that foster and sustain educator responsiveness, including contemplative practices from different traditions. He is Senior Lecturer in the Sydney School of Education and Social Work, University of Sydney.

EVE MAYES Eve Mayes is a Senior Research Fellow at Research for Educational Impact (REDI) at Deakin University, Australia. Her work centres around student voice and activism, climate justice education, and affective and participatory methodologies. Eve is currently working on the Australian Research Council-funded project: Striking Voices: Australian school-aged students' climate justice activism. Eve's book *The Politics of Voice in Education* (2023) is a simultaneous critique and affirmation of the contemporary logics of student voice in educational reform. She has ten years of experience as an English and English as an Additional Language Teacher in government secondary schools in Australia.

IAN MENTER Ian Menter is a Fellow of the Academy of Social Sciences in the UK and was President of the British Educational Research Association (BERA), 2013–15 and is also a past-President of the Scottish Educational Research Association. He is Emeritus Professor of Teacher Education and Emeritus Fellow of Kellogg College, at the University of Oxford. He previously worked at the Universities of Glasgow, the West of Scotland, London Metropolitan, the West of England and Gloucestershire. Before that he was a primary school teacher in Bristol, England. He is now a Visiting Professor at three UK universities. His main research interests are in research, policy and practice in teacher education, including comparative studies of this topic.

LINDA O'BRIEN Linda O'Brien (AM) is a retired Principal, School Leadership for the NSW Department of Education. She was the Principal of Granville Boys High School, 2008–2019 and the Deputy Principal; Head Teacher

English at Punchbowl Boys High School, from 2002 to 2008. She has taught in high schools, primary schools and TAFE in NSW and in Queensland. She has served as on various not-for-profit boards and was the Founder and Chairperson of the Bali International School. She completed a Doctor of Education in 2017 at Western Sydney University entitled 'All in the Game of School – Building a socially cohesive school'. She was granted a Member of the Order of Australia in 2013 for Innovation in secondary education and services to the community.

ALAN REID Alan Reid AM is Professor Emeritus of Education at the University of South Australia where he has held a number of positions including Dean of Education, Director of Research Centres, and Professor of Education. He publishes widely in such areas as curriculum, education policy and the history and politics of public education; and has been a key figure in some significant policy developments at the state and national levels. His most recent book – *Changing Australian Education: How Policy is taking us backwards and what can be done about it* – was published by Routledge in 2019. Alan is currently researching a history of democracy in South Australia.

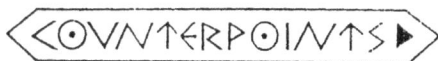

Studies in Criticality

Series Editor
Shirley R. Steinberg

Counterpoints publishes the most compelling and imaginative books being written in Education and Cultural Studies today. Grounded on the theoretical advances in critical theory, feminism, and postcolonialism in the last two decades of the twentieth century, Counterpoints engages the meaning of these innovations in various forms of educational expression. Committed to the proposition that theoretical literature should be accessible to a variety of audiences, the series insists that its authors avoid esoteric and jargonistic languages that transform educational scholarship into an elite discourse for the initiated. Scholarly work matters only to the degree it affects consciousness and practice at multiple sites. The editorial policy of *Counterpoints* is based on these principles and the ability of scholars to break new ground, to open new conversations, to go where educators have never gone before.

For additional information about this series or for the submission of manuscripts, please contact:

Shirley R. Steinberg, Series Editor
msgramsci@gmail.com

To order other books in this series, please contact our Customer Service Department:

peterlang@presswarehouse.com (within the U.S.)
orders@peterlang.com (outside the U.S.)

Or browse online by series:

www.peterlang.com

www.ingramcontent.com/pod-product-compliance
Lightning Source LLC
Chambersburg PA
CBHW050614280326
41932CB00016B/3039